HOW TO TRAIN FOR TRACK and FIELD

Techniques of the Champions

PETER HILDRETH

Foreword
by Louis J. Fisher

ARC BOOKS INC.

Second Printing 1965

Published by ARC BOOKS, Inc.
219 Park Avenue South New York N.Y. 10003

© PETER HILDRETH 1962 , 1963

Library of Congress Catalog Card No.: 62-20295

Printed in The United States of America

Foreword

by Louis J. Fisher, President
Amateur Athletic Union of the United States

There have been many books written on track and field techniques. In fact, a majority of the technical books on the subject actually devote a small portion of the book to training techniques.

It has been impressive to read of the ideas that Peter Hildreth—himself an outstanding trackman in both competition in Great Britain and in a score of international meetings—has incorporated in this volume.

The whole area of physical fitness has been given a new impetus in the United States with the interest expressed on many public occasions by President John F. Kennedy. Many secondary schools in the United States have given additional emphasis to the physical fitness of the pupils because of the figures that have been uncovered in studies among these pupils.

The Amateur Athletic Union of the United States has been vitally concerned with the physical fitness of the nation since its founding in 1888. In fact, one of the primary objectives anounced by the A.A.U. almost three quarters of a century ago concerned the role that the Union would play in the physical fitness effort of our nation.

Our Union has been concerned equally with conditioning for our athletes and non-athletes alike. Through the efforts of the A.A.U. communities have been made aware of the need for gymnasia, swimming pools, and large well-appointed parks and recreation grounds for the use of our youngsters.

In the last fifteen years the Amateur Athletic Union of the United States has actively promoted a physical fitness testing program based on track and field events. This program has been offered to almost 15 million youngsters between the ages of six and eighteen in that period.

Louis J. Fisher

Contents

Introduction

The approach to athletics: as a sport comprising many sports, track and field athletics presents a challenge to people of almost any aptitude or inclination. This handy-book outlines the history of twenty-one events, describes their technique and suggests training schedules. The idea of training is a big deterrent to many potential athletes who visualize a state of austerity and hardship to be entered with misgiving and shed with relief after a short time. Since so much of athletic life consists of training it is as well to establish from the outset that this nineteenth-century approach has no place in it. A sport that becomes a drudgery is not worth playing, and drudgery in any case is not conducive to the best results. At the same time it would be idle to pretend that training for athletics is a short or easy process. Peak fitness is only attained after a long and gradual ascent, but this is in itself rewarding, for improvement can be measured and compared with previous form.

The approach to training: though some athletic events are as unlike as cricket and football, the basic principle of training applies to all of them, the object being to prepare the mind and body for a specialized activity. The first law of intelligent training is that it should be gradual, and this applies not only to each outing but to the programme as a whole. The athlete must get fit, so to speak, in layers. He must first train for the basic fitness which will enable him to carry out the more intensive and specialized work appropriate to his event. For this reason a basic training

7

month and an immediate pre-season month of training has been suggested, but of course these can be extended to cover a much longer period with advantage.

The amount of training carried out depends on the athlete's condition at the outset, and also on the important and often overlooked fact that individuals vary widely as to the amount of conditioning they can usefully absorb at any time. The volume of exercise will also be affected by participation in other sports, particularly those like football and squash which involve a strenuous workout. All this points to the need for flexibility in the approach to training, so the programmes outlined in the ensuing pages should not be accepted as a rigid formula but merely as a framework which the individual can adapt to his personal needs.

Intensity of training is another matter for individual discretion and the guiding policy should certainly be a long term one. Muscles always respond better to a gradual increase in exertion, and here the vital role of warming-up must be stressed. Optimum performance is impossible without careful warming-up and one of the objectives of training is to explore the possibilities of limbering as an aid to fuller release of the athlete's reserves in competition.

Subsidiary forms of conditioning such as weight training and circuit training are recommended in the text but not elaborated, as being outside the scope of this volume. They are none the less valuable aids to fitness because in building strength they contribute to the acquisition of physical skills, the two processes being complementary to each other.

If the approach to training should be flexible so also should it be varied if the athlete is to derive the fullest value from his workouts. He should strive constantly to avoid boredom by exploring new methods and changing the scene of his activity. Unsociability is another enemy of progress.

The company of friends is a valuable stimulus in training, for athletes working together can help each other to learn more about their event, and most important, about themselves.

Specialization: the choice of an event is sometimes automatic, sometimes the outcome of experiment. Some events go naturally together, like sprinting and long jumping, and it is hoped that in reading this book the athlete will not restrict himself to the pages dealing with his favourite event. Study of the section on sprinting should in fact supplement reading on most track and field events, because speed is a component of good performance in all the jumping and throwing events. Many athletes only discover their best event after attempting several others and there is no doubt that all-round participation does promote better all-round fitness. But however true this may be, the athlete should never lose sight of the fact that the best results are ultimately achieved by complete specialization.

Health: while it is not necessary to dwell on the common-sense rules of health which are important to everyone not least the athlete in training, certain general observations on health may be useful. It is accepted that athletic training and competition can do no harm to the healthy subject but strenuous activity will always find out any latent weakness. It is wise, therefore, to take the precaution of a complete medical check-up before embarking on serious training. Regular checks will also forestall trouble from the teeth which are a frequent focus of infection and hence of poor form. Care of the feet is an obvious rule. Athlete's foot is a common condition which can now be cured either superficially or orally. Colds and other minor complaints need not curtail training though it is generally unwise to compete at a time when there is any doubt about fitness.

Injury: patience in building-up through a gradual training programme will pay big dividends not only in performance but in keeping free from injury. The risk of muscle strain can be largely reduced by thorough warming-up and by a graduated increase in training intensity. If this caution is observed the services of a masseur will be superfluous, but in the event of muscle trouble, qualified treatment should be taken at the earliest opportunity. Delay only means greater discomfort from an aggravated injury and more time lost in training. Injuries beyond those requiring simple first-aid are generally catered for at athletic meetings where medical and nursing staff usually attend in case of emergencies. It is as well to remember that more fatalities are caused in athletics through carelessness in the region of the throwing events than in any any other way.

Diet: the qualities claimed for certain patent products suggest that athletic prowess depends on what the performer eats or drinks. This is a complete fallacy. Obviously a plentiful and varied diet is essential to good health and vitality, but no special regimen will transform an athlete into a champion. The famous coach who recommended home cooking and plenty of it, put the whole question of diet for athletes into the right perspective.

The question of pre-competition meals however deserves closer study. Nervous apprehension retards digestion and many athletes find that an interval of two or three hours between eating and competing allows them to perform without discomfort. In the more punishing track events where the runner's whole body undergoes a severe ordeal, a gap of up to five hours is sometimes preferred. With these broad indications in mind, the athlete should decide which interval suits him best by noting his own feelings. The man who rises late on the morning of competition, for example, may decide that breakfast alone is sufficient. The content of the pre-race meal should of course be light. No particular food will enhance performance though glucose tablets may have a soothing effect on the worried competitor and can certainly do no harm.

Abstinence: excessive smoking and drinking are injurious to health, but moderate indulgence cannot handicap the athlete and may even be beneficial if he enjoys it.

Note: Statistics mentioned in the text represent the latest positions in 1962. American Champions (Record Holders) are given as of July 1962. Reigning title holders listed from the European and Empire Games are from 1958 and the Olympic Games in 1960.

PART ONE

Sprinting

100 YARDS   100 METRES (109.36) yards)

U. S. CHAMPION 100 YARDS   Frank Budd (at New York,
1961) 9.2 secs

EMPIRE CHAMPION 100 YARDS   Keith Gardner (Jamaica)
9.4 secs.

EUROPEAN CHAMPION 100 METRES Armin Hary (Germany)
10.3 secs

OLYMPIC CHAMPION 100 METRES Armin Hary (Germany)
10.2 secs

(Approximate time differential between 100 yards and 100
metres is 0.8 sec)

THE first acceptable instance of 'even' time being broken
for 100 yards was in the A.A.U. Championships at Washington in 1890, when John Owen Junior won the American
title in 9.8 secs. The feat was not accomplished by an
Englishman on native soil until Willie Applegarth returned
9.8 secs at Stamford Bridge on the 20th June 1914.

A decade elapsed before another Englishmen attained
world sprint fame: Harold Abrahams won the Olympic
100 metres at Paris in 1924 and equalled the Olympic record
of 10.6 secs in heat, semi-final, and final. The unofficial title
of world's fastest human was held at that time by a highly
muscular Californian named Charlie Paddock, who tied the
world record for 100 yards six times at 9.6 secs between
1921 and 1926, and also attached his name to the 100 metres
best in 10.4 secs. Since improvements of less than two-tenths
were not then recognized, it required 9.4 secs to remove
Paddock's name from the record books in 1930 and another

American, Frank Wykoff, to speed the 100 yards in that time.

In the mid-thirties the track world was electrified by the exploits of a smooth-running   U.S. flyer named Jesse Owens, who twice tied the 100 yards record and made the 100 metres his sole property in 10.2 secs. In 1936 Owens set the seal on his immortality by capturing the Olympic 100 metres title at Berlin. His winning series in the Games, of 10.3, 10.2, 10.4, 10.3, is an aggregate unsurpassed in Olympic history.

The 100 yards record was reduced to 9.3 secs in 1948 by another white American, Mel Patton, who sustained a surprise Olympic defeat at Wembley by Harrison Dillard. Though better known as a hurdler, Dillard equalled the Olympic 100 metres record of 10.3 secs.

At home, Applegarth's ancient record remained intact until the advent of Peter Radford in 1958. Radford made three successive inroads on the United Kingdom best, racing 9.4 secs in 1960 and also several times tying the 100 metres best of 10.3 secs standing to the credit of Roy Sandstrom. This time also sufficed Radford to gain an Olympic bronze medal. It was equalled again by David Jones in 1961.

The thirteen-year-old 100 yard world record had been equalled by eleven runners before it was finally clipped to 9.2 secs by the American runner, Frank Budd, in 1961. The 100 metres best reached the hard and even level of 10.0 secs in 1960. This mark was set by the Olympic champion, Armin Hary, and equalled within a month by the Canadian negro, Harry Jerome.

Sprinting is running in top gear, the fullest form of a purely natural exercise. Apart from warlike contests, it is probably the oldest form of competitive physical activity. Since by definition no artificial skills are involved in sprinting, technique does not play a major role in it. Improvement lies rather in perfecting natural movements by repeated practice, and by increased muscular capacity, which is also the outcome of constant practice.

A famous coach once said that a man can sprint a lot of different ways and still be right. By this he meant that every sprinter will tend to fall into a style suited to his own physical make-up and posture. It is safe to add that whatever their style, the fundamental ingredients of locomotion are the same. A study of any good sprinter in action will show that he is making full use of his limbs in à complete and powerful range of movement. He is, in effect, trying to get the maximum out of every stride.

The first pre-requisite of powerful movement is muscular strength. Though they come in all sizes, the best sprinters are men in whom muscular power rates high in proportion to body weight. David Sime is of heroic build, standing 6 ft. 2½ in. and weighing nearly 180 lbs. Jesse Owens and Armin Hary are of medium physique standing rather less than 6 ft. and weighing between 155 and 165 lbs. Mike Agostini of Trinidad and Ira Murchinson of America, both finalists in the Melbourne Olympic 100 metres, are under 5 ft. 8 in. in height. Though varied in stature, all these great sprinters have a high power–weight ratio.

The second cardinal factor in sprinting is that power must be channelled into efficient action. This fluency is not so much the result of deliberate rehearsal, but of good muscular condition derived from hard and persevering training. It has been pointed out that training should always be a gradual process. In sprinting, where explosive effort is demanded, it is more than ever vital to tune up the muscles

in easy stages. Full pressure work should not be attempted
without limbering-up thoroughly, the hardest exercise
being reserved for the end of the outing.

Basic training

For the sprints this should be directed at building a found-
ation of general fitness on which a more intensive programme
of specific training can be undertaken. Basic training can
take several forms, the first being simply free running.

Free running: this is sometimes known by the Swedish
word 'fartlek' meaning speed-play. It consists of running at
will over an indefinite distance and at varying speeds, with
stretches of fast striding interspersed as the muscles get
warmer. The sprinter can run in this way for perhaps three
to five miles in all.

Free Exercises are recommended to develop suppleness
and mobility in the thighs, hips and shoulders to facilitate
a full range of movement in sprinting. Such exercises as
windmill arm swinging, leg swinging laterally and longitudinally, trunk rotating, feet apart splits, wrestler's bridge
(back bending), are ideal.

Resistance Exercises develop power in the sprint levers,
that is in the arms and legs, and in the body generally.
Weight and circuit training are admirable for this purpose.
If facilities are not available, such exercises as press-ups,
sit-ups, chinning the bar, medicine-ball throwing, squat
jumping and step running are other forms of resistance
exercise which serve the same purpose.

Winders are preliminary track runs in which the sprinter
sets out to cover a distance at an ever increasing speed,
approaching his top speed only at the end of his run. This
is a good way of breaking in the muscles gradually for full-
speed running.

Intervals are repeated runs over a pre-determined distance with walking or jogging interspersed for recovery.

Hill running is a form of resistance and stamina training which most runners perform at some stage in their training. It is a useful basic strengthening exercise for sprinters.

Though a sprint race should always be thought of as a composite whole in practice, it is convenient in writing to deal with it in phases.

Figure 1

The Start: after many years of evolution through various forms of running, lying, and standing starts, and experiments with mechanical starting gates, the most satisfactory form of getaway yet devised is from the crouch position, with the report of a gun as the signal to start. This was first introduced about 1887, though it is interesting to note that John Owen's record of 9.8 secs was accomplished from a standing start.

At the command 'on your marks' the sprinter takes up the position illustrated in figure 1. The shoulders should be over the hands which are slightly wider apart than the shoulders for better control in the 'set' position. Most athletes use a finger-tip support on the marks, but Armin Hary, Olympic 100 metres champion, prefers a thumb and knuckle support. When, after careful experiment, the sprinter has established the position which suits him best, he should measure and note the spacings between each foot and the line. An average spread is 16 in. from the line to the front foot, and 30 in. to the back foot.

At the command 'set' he tilts forward, poised now on toes and finger-tips, to a point just short of toppling, which he can hold comfortably for about five seconds (Fig. 2). An interval of between one and two seconds in the 'set' is average, though it may well be less, and is sometimes more.

Figure 2

Any attempt at anticipating the gun will probably lead to unsteadiness or to a break. The best policy is simply to listen for the gun. If all other thoughts are excluded, the bang should trigger off an immediate response, launching the sprinter into his stride with a powerful drive from arms and legs.

Acceleration: some sprinters are seen to be fast over 15 or 20 yards, and this early speed is desirable providing it is not cultivated to the detriment of a full range of acceleration. This does not depend on leg speed but on strength. Sprint cadence varies hardly at all in the course of a race. Speed grows with stride length which stretches from perhaps two feet at the start to about seven feet in full stride. The sprinter should concentrate on running from the blocks and avoid cultivating choppy opening strides which may be effective for 20 yards but can inhibit his overall progress to top speed. Armin Hary is said to be in his running after three strides. With the head held in normal alignment, an upright sprinting position is reached after about 30 yards. Top speed, 24 m.p.h. among the best sprinters, is attained after about 60 yards.

The Race: it has been proved that top speed is a brief stage of perhaps no more than 30 yards. This is because muscles working at full pressure accumulate fatigue at thirty times the normal rate. Tension and struggle will of course limit this stage still further, so relaxed effort is essential. The world records of Jesse Owens and Mel Patton were reported to have been performed with apparent ease, suggesting that if they had really tried, they might have run faster. In fact the absence of tension was the secret of success. Had they striven harder they would probably have moved less swiftly.

The Finish: the sprinter must concentrate on his own lane throughout the race; any movement of the head will cause him to sway off course and lose ground. The rules state that the result of a race is judged by reference to that part of the runner's torso which crosses the line first. A few extra inches can be gained by dipping forward from the waist on the last stride through the tape. Alternative to the 'dip' is the 'shrug' finish, where the torso is turned on the last stride presenting the shoulder first. A combination of the two achieves the maximum advantage that can be gained in final reach for the line.

These techniques should never be used unless thoroughly practised. In the ordinary way it is better to treat the race as though it ends several yards past the tape, and maintain the pressure right through it. Remember that the 1932 Olympic 100 metres final at Los Angeles was won by Eddie Tolan from Ralph Metcalf by only two inches, so every detail of the race should be studied with a view to achieving the fullest expenditure of energy between gun and tape.

Sample warming-up schedule. Before track training the following warming-up should be carried out. Half-mile jogging, free exercises, 3–4 winders 80–100 yards. A lap or two of jogging should be taken as a tapering-off process after training.

MONTH 1

Training programme for one week.

1st day. Free running 30 minutes, including stretches of striding up to 150 yards. Taper off with half a mile jogging to complete a distance of about 3–5 miles.

2nd day. Track training. 4 × 150 yards or 6 × 60 yards intervals, walking back each time.

3rd day. Hill running session. Select steep gradient of 50–80 yards on road or country. 5–10 runs with accentuated knee lift and piston arm action.

4th day. Weight or circuit training if available, otherwise repeat free running session.

MONTH 2

Training programme for one week.

1st day. Track training. Set starting blocks. 3–5 starts driving hard for 20–30 yards and easing up gradually.

4 × 100 yards fast striding on the turn, hugging the line, walk to complete a lap each time.

2nd day. Fast striding runs at 50–75–100–150–100–75–50, walking back each time for recovery and trying to make the last two runs flat out.

3rd day. Set blocks for competitive starts. Take 2–3 sets of 3 starts over either 50 or 60 yards. Pause between each start for better concentration and rest for 10 minutes between each set of starts. If possible time the runs and study the times as an aid to establishing how much running precedes optimum performance.

4th day. 5–10 fast striding runs of 100 yards. Walk back each time and study the spike marks. An even parallel set of prints indicates balanced running meaning energy converted into effective forward drive.

5th day. Weight or circuit training.

Competition

By the end of the second month of training, the sprinter should be fit enough to begin racing. As the more important competitions will take place later, the early races can serve as a final pipe-opener, bringing him to peak form at the height of the season. With the accent now on sharpening the edge of speed, the type of training should be as outlined in the programme for the first and third days of Month 2. Assuming that competition will normally be on a Saturday, training will take place on perhaps three or four days, with rest on Friday and Sunday.

On the day of competition: arrange to be at the track at least one hour before the start. Study the programme and timetable and report to the competitor's steward, collecting your number and find out which heat you are in. Pin your number on your vest and make sure that you have no other distraction for 45 minutes before the race so that you can concentrate on warming-up. Be at the start ten minutes before your race, complete with blocks and nails. If possible study the starter's interval in previous heats so that a quick gun will not catch you off your guard. Take one practice start off your blocks. Strip at the last moment. When on the marks think only of the gun; when you hear it, think only of winning.

After the race make an immediate post-mortem with a view to eliminating weaknesses during the coming weeks of training. If another race is due return to the dressing room and lie down, coming out again ten minutes before the next start to prepare.

220 YARDS   200 METRES (218.72 yards)

U.S. CHAMPION 200 YARDS Ray Norton (at Berkley, Cal., 1960) 20.6 secs

EMPIRE CHAMPION 220 YARDS Tom Robinson (Bahamas) 21.0 secs

EUROPEAN CHAMPION 200 METRES Manfred Germar (Germany)   21.0 secs

OLYMPIC CHAMPION 200 METRES   Livio Berruti (Italy) 20.5 secs

(Approximate time differential between 200 metres and 220 yards is 0.1 secs.)

Only two weeks after his 100 yards record in 1914, Willie Applegarth ran 220 yards on a full turn at Stamford Bridge in 21.2 secs, a time previously accomplished in track history only on straight courses. Since the estimated advantage afforded by a straight course is four-tenths, Charlie Paddock's 1921 world record of 20.8 secs did not perhaps constitute a net improvement. It fell to another American, Roland Locke, to make genuine progress with a 20.5 clocking in 1926, but as times were then registered to the nearest fifth, this was listed as 20.6 secs.

The next record tenant was the illustrious Jesse Owens, whose 20.3 secs was set on the 25th May 1935, the same afternoon as his world records for 100 yards, 220 yards hurdles, and long jump. Owens also took the Olympic 200 metres title in 20.7 secs, which remained an Olympic record for twenty years. The slender and light-footed Mel Patton shaved another tenth from the 220 record in 1948, and made amends for his failure in the Olympic 100 metres by winning the 200.

Dave Sime was responsible for two reductions in the 220 record, racing a level 20.0 secs at Sanger, California in 1956. Like all previous holders of the straight record, Sime was automatically credited with the same time at the slightly shorter 200 metres distance. The 1956 Melbourne Olympic title went to Bobbie Morrow in 20.6 secs, with yet another American, Andy Stanfield, clocking 20.7 secs in second place, a time which had enabled him to win a gold medal at Helsinki four years earlier.

The United Kingdom's best stood in Applegarth's name until 1958 when Peter Radford recorded 21.0 secs. In 1960 Radford became the first non-American in forty-six years to hold a world furlong record by sprinting 20.5 secs on a full turn at Aldersley Stadium, Wolverhampton. The I.A.A.F. now lists separate versions of this record on straight and turn courses. With two Americans, Ray Norton and Stone Johnson bracketed with Radford as holders of the 200 metres turn record, the Olympic victory of Italy's Livio Berruti at Rome was as unexpected as it was brilliant. The lithe Italian left no doubt of his supremacy by equalling the world record in both semi-final and final, within the space of two hours.

The ability to win Olympic sprint doubles enhances the claims of certain performers to a special place in the history of sprinting. The holders of this rare distinction are Ralph Craig (1912), Percy Williams (1928), Eddie Tolan (1932), Jesse Owens (1936), and Bobbie Morrow (1956), the second named being a Canadian and the rest Americans.

Most sprinters compete over both 100 and 220 yards and it should be possible on the training outlined in the previous section to attempt either distance without difficulty. There

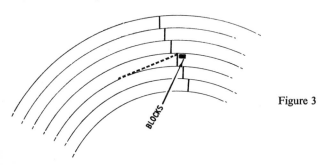

Figure 3

are certain aspects of sprinting however, which are peculiar to the furlong and these require special attention and training. The most important arise out of the fact that the race is normally run on a turn, the standard course being half a 440 yard circuit, starting at the end of one straight, and finishing at the end of the next. This is the case in all championship 220 yards events, though straight courses do exist at several American arenas and at a few in this country.

Starting on the turn is the first point to be studied. Since the runners keep to their lanes, the starts are in echelon, or staggered, and this means that they are actually situated on the curve of the track (Fig. 3). The orthodox practice is for the blocks to be set at the outer edge of the lane so that the opening strides can be run in a straight line, approaching the curve at a tangent. It was observed at Rome however that the Olympic champion, Livio Berruti, preferred to set his blocks on the inner edge of his lane, giving himself a slightly shorter distance to run. The relative merit of these two methods are debatable, but the sprinter himself should experiment with both and satisfy himself that he has chosen the method which suits him best.

Sprinting on the turn is a delicate skill requiring regular practice. The estimated cost in time through impetus lost in negotiating a 180 degree turn is four-tenths of a second. Only impeccable banking can prevent this delay from being longer, and frequent turn runs in training are indicated. The only adjustment to normal sprint action is a slight inward lean of the body. The head should be held in normal alignment and the arms worked as usual. Fluent turn running is assisted by another important factor in 220 yards technique:

The Coast or float which, as the name implies, is a stage of the race in which the sprinter allows himself to free-wheel. This does not mean that he slows down, but that in reaching full speed after 50 or 60 yards, he eases pressure imperceptibly. This has the effect of reducing muscle tension and delaying the onset of fatigue. Though a slight loss of impetus may at first be suffered in learning the coast, the sprinter will find that as he gains experience, his effort will carry further at full speed because he is economizing. There is no short cut to learning the coast. Every opportunity of acquiring fluency of movement in training should be taken. When doing repetition runs he should concentrate on holding his form after fatigue has taken the edge off his speed. This is particularly important in furlong running at the finish.

The Finish of a 220 is often as exacting as that of a quarter-mile. Races are won or lost more often in the last 30 yards than in any other stage. The tendency to struggle must be checked. Control and balance are essential and emphasis should be placed on a powerful arm action and a final drive for a point well beyond the line. The head should be held in normal alignment and a dip or shrug finish reserved for the last stride across the line. The danger of lunging from two or three strides out cannot be over-emphasized. Loss of balance and hence of speed can only result from a mis-timed dip.

Special training for 220 yards

Modern sprinting has become so specialized that it is almost impossible for one man to succeed in the top flight at both distances. In the Rome Olympics only one sprinter reached the final of both 100 and 200 metres, the American runner Ray Norton ; he finished last in each. It is advisable to decide well in advance of an important competition which distance is preferred.

The 220-yard specialist should undertake some over-distance runs and occasional runs up to 440 yards will do no harm. Study of the table on page 37 showing intermediate times of great quarter-milers, reveals that some of them approached their best 220-yard times on the way to completing 440 yards. This was because their coast was good and carried them smoothly through the 220 mark.

Sample training week for 220 man

1st day. Starts and short dashes with 100-yard men.

2nd day. 2–3 time trials over 100 yards on the turn.

3rd day. Starts and one good run over 300 yards, timed at the 220 mark.

4th day. 3–4 crescendo runs over 250 yards, run at a fast striding speed and trying to hold form while accelerating over the last 50.

5th day. Starts and short dashes with 100-yard men.

On the day of the competition: in addition to the routine preparations outlined in the section on 100 yards, the 220-yard man must make a point of doing some of his warming-up on the turn used for his race. Turns vary, and it helps to get the feel of your turn before racing. As the echelon starts are fanned out over a distance of about 15 yards, the starter may give his orders through a microphone. Make sure that you can hear him, particularly if you are in an outer lane.

Do not allow yourself to slack on the turn, the others will soon catch up as the echelon resolves. In the straight, concentrate on holding your form. It may help to develop some uniform thought pattern as did Jesse Owens who thought only of keeping his feet off the ground. After the race make an immediate post-mortem. In particular examine your tracks to see how you took the turn.

4 × 110 YARDS RELAY
4 × 100 METRES RELAY (437.44 yards)

U.S. CHAMPIONS 4 × 110 yards	(W. Wilson, E. Southern, H. Gainey, R. Alspaugh, at Modesto, Cal. 1959) 39.6 secs
EMPIRE CHAMPIONS 4 × 110 yards	England (Radford, Sandstrom, Segal, Breaker) 40.7 secs
EUROPEAN CHAMPIONS 4 × 100 metres	Germany (Futterer, Mahlendorf, Hary, Germar) 40.2 secs

OLYMPIC CHAMPIONS	Germany (Cullman, Mahlendorf,
4 × 100 metres	Hary, Lauer) 39.5 secs

(Approximate time differential between 400 metres and 440 yards is 0.3 secs.)

Relay racing originated in the United States, the first important relay meeting having been the Pennsylvania Relay Carnival in 1893. The sprint relay was not introduced to the Olympic programme until 1912 at Stockholm when a United Kingdom team, D. H. Jacobs, H. H. Macintosh, Victor D'Arcy, and Willie Applegarth, won gold medals in 42.4 secs. Another British team composed of Harold Abrahams, Walter Rangeley, Lancelot Royle, and Bill Nichol, briefly held the world record at 42.0 secs in a heat of the Olympic 4 × 100 metres relay at Paris in 1924. This mark was matched within minutes by a Dutch team and reduced the next day by the American team, who won the final in 41.0 secs, a fifth ahead of the British quartet.

An unbroken run of American Olympic success over the next 24 years was briefly disturbed in 1948 when the Archer, team, Alistair McCorquodale, Jack Gregory, Jack British and Ken Jones, were awarded gold medals on the disqualification of the United States squad. A study of the film proved the Americans blameless however, and the gold medals were duly handed over to the rightful recipients. Barney Ewell, Lorenzo Wright, Harrison Dillard and Mel Patton who had run 40.6 secs. The most prolific Olympic relay sprinter was perhaps Frank Wykoff who figured in winning American teams in 1928, 1932, and 1936. In the last, at Berlin, he completed a quartet comprising Jesse Owens, Ralph Metcalfe, and Foy Draper who set a world record of 39.8 secs. This mark was untouched until 1956 when another American team, Ira Murchison, Leamon King, Thane Baker and Bobbie Morrow recorded 39.5 secs.

The American monopoly of Olympic sprint relays terminated at Rome where, though first past the post, they were disqualified on a first takeover infringement, and the German team, named above, took the gold medals in 39.5 secs. This mishap also advanced the British team, Peter Radford, David Jones, David Segal and Nick Whitehead, to bronze medal status in 40.2 secs. The 4 × 110 yards world record reached 39.6 secs in 1959 and stands to the credit of a team from the University of Texas, U. S. A., W. Wilson, E. Southern, H. Gainey, and P. Alspaugh.

Relay racing is an absorbing addition to the sprinter's repertoire, demanding personal skill together with team discipline. It has become so popular in modern athletics that most competitions include a sprint relay and since it is usually staged at the end of the programme, the result of a match may depend on it.

The day when the best team of sprinters always won the relay has passed. A successful team must have worked together for many months and perfected the takeover precision which enables the baton to travel the course in the shortest time possible with their aggregate speeds. This was evident at Rome where the American quartet, Ray Norton, Stone Johnson, Frank Budd, and Dave Sime, though unquestionably the fastest team, were disqualified for crossing the first takeover zone. All four had been finalists in individual sprints, all except Budd were current world-record holders. In contrast the Russian four, none of whom had reached even a semi-final of an individual sprint, came

through in the relay to win silver medals in the highly
impressive time of 39.8 secs.

Choice of Leg: the first problem to be considered in
training a sprint relay team is the allocation of stages to
the chosen four. It is usual for the fastest individual to take
the first leg because he will be carrying the baton farthest.
The changeover zone extends for eleven yards (or ten metres
in a 4 × 100 metres event) on either side of the line ending
the stage. He will therefore cover 110 yards plus about
8 yards into the farther stage, allowing a scant 3 yards for
safe delivery to the outgoing man. By the same calculation
the second and third runners will carry the baton about 110
yards each and the last man 102 yards only (See Fig. 4).

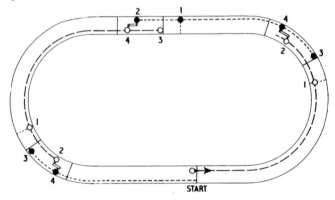

Figure 4

Theoretically, time trials over these distances should
guide the decision as to running order, but since the first
and third legs are run on the turn, ability to corner must be
considered too. In the British Olympic team at Rome,
Peter Radford's selection for the first leg was automatic,
based on his superior speed. David Segal, best at 200 metres

running, took the third leg on the turn. David Jones took over from Radford on the second leg, while the slowest, Nick Whitehead, ran fourth.

Starting: only the first runner starts from a crouch position, and since he is holding the baton, he must adopt a grip which will give him sufficient support in the set position. The baton should be gripped by one or two fingers, leaving two fingers and thumb for ground support (Fig. 5). At least half the baton should be exposed for the grasp of the next runner at takeover. The remaining three runners

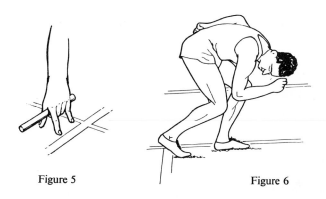

Figure 5   Figure 6

will start from a semi-crouch stance (Fig. 6) enabling them to watch the incoming runner under their shoulder.

The takeover: a perfect change would involve the baton passing from hand to hand with both runners moving at top speed. This is not quite possible because the outgoing man has only about 20 yards in which to gather impetus. From his semi-crouch stance, he watches for the incoming man to hit the check mark. Then he turns and sprints hard for eight strides before dropping his hand to receive the baton. It is

essential to count these strides because that is the maximum
distance he can travel with the use of both arms.

The check mark is usually a crease in the track, white
lines are not permitted. Its exact situation can only be
determined by trial and error between the two runners
concerned who must have rehearsed their routine at full
speed.

Baton Passing: the most efficient method of baton
passing, and also the most difficult, is the alternate hand
change. The first sprinter holds the baton in his left hand,

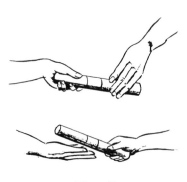

Figure 7

the second receives in his right and so on. The third runner,
receiving in his left hand, must make allowances for the
incoming man's approach on the inside edge of his lane by
taking up his stance on the outside of the lane.

There are two methods of receiving the baton (Fig. 7).
The hand can be extended palm uppermost for a downward
delivery, and palm down for an upward pass. As stated,
the receiver must make full use of both arms in gaining

momentum for eight strides before dropping his hand into position to grasp the baton. If the check mark drill is accurate he should not have to look round. With the baton in his grasp, he must sprint hard for the whole of his stage. If the baton does not project sufficiently from his hand to ensure a safe transfer, it may be necessary for him to work his hand down a little before parting with the baton.

Special training for relays: obviously assimilation of these techniques requires religious practice. It should be possible for drill on such details as starting from the semi-crouch stance and baton-passing at speed, to be carried out by members of a team in pairs. These exercises could form part of warming-up or as a variant to repetition work. It must be made quite clear however that relay performance can only be perfected by a team running the full course at top speed in training. Obviously the correct sequence cannot be reproduced in any other way. Approach adjustments can be made and accurate check marks established. A full-dress rehearsal should take place at least once a week, and might well form the high point of a training session for the chosen four with observers posted at each takeover to report the point at which the baton changes hands. I can recall watching the British Olympic sprint relay team run three practice courses the day before taking part in the preliminaries of the 4 × 100 metres relay in which they won bronze medals.

440 YARDS   400 METRES (437.44 yards)

U.S. CHAMPION 440 YARDS Glenn Davis at Berkley, Cal.
1958)   45.7 secs
EMPIRE CHAMPION 440 YARDS   Milkha Singh (India)
46.6 secs
EUROPEAN CHAMPION 400 METRES John Wrighton (G.B.)
46.3 secs

OLYMPIC CHAMPION 400 METRES   Otis Davis (U.S.A.)

44.9 secs

(Approximate time differential between 400 metres and 440 yards is 0.3 secs.)

In 1881 a diminutive American named Lawrence Myers, who had already become the first human to break 50.0 secs for 440 yards, ran the distance in 48.6 secs at Birmingham. This time was eclipsed after five years at Harvard University where, with aid of a straight course, but handicapped by the loss of his left shoe, Wendell Baker recorded 47.6 secs.

The first important British landmark was set by the Cambridge blue H. C. Lennox Tindall in 1889 with a time of 48.6 secs, an A.A.A. Championship record until 1937. The 1908 Olympic Games at White City was the scene of a unique 400 metres walkover when Lt. Wyndham Halswell collected a solo gold medal after three American rivals had withdrawn in sympathy with a disqualified colleague. A more satisfying victory was that of the Scot, Eric Liddell, at Paris in 1924. Choosing the 400 metres because his religious principles excluded running in 100-metre heats on the Sabbath, Liddell stormed round in the outside lane for a world record of 47.6 secs.

In 1932 the pace of quarter-miling was drastically modernized by a spare bespectacled American named Ben Eastman who axed a whole second from the linear record with 46.4 secs. This also passed as a 400 metres best for lack of additional timekeepers at that point. The same year Eastman was outraced by his compatriot Bill Carr in the Olympic final with a world's best of 46.2 secs. The Berlin Olympic final in 1936 saw Britain's closest approach to the front since Liddell, with Godfrey Brown a gallant second in 46.7 secs to the American negro Archie Williams, who had recently been responsible for a tenth improvement on Carr's record.

The forging of one lap history after the war fell to Jamaicans, the greatest of whom was Herb McKenley with 46.0 secs for the linear record and 45.9 secs for the metric. Like Eastman however, McKenley was over the top at the Olympics and went down to the long-striding Arthur Wint in the Wembley 400 metres final. A third Jamaican, George Rhoden, deprived McKenley of individual gold medal honours for the second time in 1952 with 45.9 secs.

In 1955 the 400 metres record remained negro property when America's Louis Jones benefited by the rarefied atmosphere of Mexico City at 7,000 ft. to clock 45.4 secs. A year later he confirmed his greatness with a sea-level 45.2 secs in the U.S. Olympic Tryouts at Los Angeles. Even this seemingly irreducible time proved mortal at Rome in 1960 when Otis Davis broke another barrier with 44.9 secs, a mark shared in second place by Germany's Carl Kaufmann.

Godfrey Brown's United Kingdom best remained until 1958 when Surgeon-Lieutenant John Wrighton became European Champion in 46.3 secs. This was reduced to 46.1 secs by the Loughborough College student, Robbie Brightwell, when failing narrowly to qualify for the Olympic final at Rome. An out-of-the-blue performance by the Oxford undergraduate, Adrian Metcalfe in July 1961, brought him a new United Kingdom record of 45.8 secs at Oslo.

The pace of modern quarter-miling leaves no room for doubt that the event is really a sprint. Most great quarter-milers are in fact first-class 100- and 220-yard men who have extended their repertoire, only a few being half-milers who have come down. The student of quarter-miling should therefore treat this section as supplementary to the sections on the shorter distances.

Obviously the cardinal difference between the 440 and 220 yards lies in the fact that effort has to be distributed over twice the distance. It has already been shown that the range of any man's top speed is very limited and that this is due to the high rate at which fatigue accumulates in muscles working at full pressure. The 440 yards is the longest running distance in which top speed is involved. In longer runs the pace is always such that the athlete does recover, at least in part, from the effects of fatigue while he is running. In the 440 yards sprint he is running into almost total debt.

Sprint action in the 440 yards must therefore be the most economical rhythm that is compatible with a near flat-out effort. Since he is not concerned with getting the maximum out of every stride as in the 100 yards, he can cover the ground with a slightly less vigorous knee lift and arm action. A freer pivot at the hips and shoulders will make for smoother coasting and counter the tendency to bunch up, particularly as he works to sustain the tempo beyond the 300 yards mark.

Pace Judgement is a vital factor in 440 yards running. It is well known that distance runners study lap times in an attempt to cultivate even pace. In the quarter-mile, even pace is not employed in quite the same way, but study of the intermediate times is a useful guide to the right kind of distribution of effort. In this connexion we can do no better than review the performances of record holders in this event.

Year	Name	Country	1st 220 secs	2nd 220 secs	440 secs
1900	Maxie Long	U.S.A.	22.8	25.0	47.8
1924	Eric Liddell	G.B.	22.2	25.4	47.6m
1928	Emerson Spencer	U.S.A.	22.0	25.0	47.0m
1932	Ben Eastman	,,	21.4	25.0	46.4
1947	Herb McKenley	Jamaica	20.9	25.4	46.3
1948	Herb McKenley	,,	21.0	25.0	46.0
1950	George Rhoden	,,	20.9	24.9	45.8m
1952	George Rhoden	,,	22.2	23.7	45.9m
1952	Herb McKenley	,,	22.7	23.2	45.9m
1956	Louis Jones	U.S.A.	21.3	23.9	45.2m
1960	Otis Davis	,,	21.7	23.2	44.9m
1960	Carl Kaufmann	Germany	21.8	23.1	44.9m

m = 400 metres race

The first observation to be made from these figures is that the first half of the race is invariably run faster than the second. Right up until 1956, records were broken exclusively by virtue of a faster first 220 yards, the second 220 being as slow in 1950 as it had been in 1900. The extremes of pace distribution employed by Herb McKenley are of particular interest. In his early records he was fading at the finish. At Helsinki in 1952, however, he entered the final straight in the Olympic final about four yards down on George Rhoden and failed to catch him only by inches. Since Rhoden had spread his effort wisely he was able to hold off McKenley's finishing burst, but it is likely that the latter would have won had he been level with Rhoden after 200 metres in 22.2 secs.

Louis Jones found a medium between the reckless sprinting of his two predecessors in the record books, and the earlier champions, but it remained for Otis Davis to develop a fresh aspect of the race. He appeared at Rome to make his strongest effort from 200 metres to 300 metres and was fading in the last 50 metres, being nearly caught by Kaufmann on the tape. Kaufmann's judgement was probably nearer the optimum and it may well be that further reductions will come from him.

The opinion of Godfrey Brown deserves the closest attention in resolving a method of 440-yard running in the light of this history. Brown held that while the first half was bound to be faster than the second, deceleration should not be too steep, but gradual, like clockwork running down. He also said that the strongest finisher, that is the man most likely to win, will be the man who slows down least.

Month 1

Training programme for one week.

1st day. Free running 30 minutes, including stretches of striding up to 300 yards.

2nd day. Track training. Interval running 4 × 220 yards or 4 × 440 yards, jogging a similar distance between.

3rd day. Hill running with 100- and 220-yard men.

4th day. Weight training or circuit training if available, otherwise repeat free running.

Month 2

Training programme for one week.

1st day. Starts and short dashes with 100-yard men.

2nd day. Repetition running over 220 yards in 24–25 secs (suggested time for 50 secs quarter-miler). Run 3–4 times as though for the first half of a race. Rest 5 minutes each time.

3rd day. Crescendo runs over 300 yards with 220-yard men.

4th day. 1–2 runs over 660 yards at about 90 secs (for a 50 secs man).

The quarter-miler should pay careful attention to his turn running. If he races occasionally over 220 yards he will gain experience of this, but since in the 440 he has to go round two full turns he therefore has twice as much to gain by smooth banking.

Another important factor is the echelon start. Here the stagger is about seven yards between each lane and the runner in the sixth lane about 40 yards away from the inside man at the start. It is therefore vital that he should know the pace which he can sustain and be able to run out on his own without fear of reaching the straight out of touch with his rivals. The runner who can win from the outside lane, as did George Rhoden in the 1952 Olympic final, and Louis Jones when setting his 1956 world record, has mastered one lap judgement.

Competition

Assuming that he will race on a Saturday, the quarter-miler will probably train on three or four other days, the kind of work he does corresponding to the second and third days in Month 2. Should he find that he lacks stamina in competition, some over-distance runs could be included in the next week's training, but in general the accent should be on speed, the weekly race being sufficient stamina training in itself.

On the day of competition study all routine preparations suggested for 100- and 220-yard men. Take particular care in finding out the qualifying conditions in the heats. In the 440 fastest losers are sometimes taken for the final, so it may be necessary to go all out in the heat. If you feel sick after your heat it often helps to take glucose tablets. Walk around until the uneasiness settles, then rest in the dressing room.

4 × 440 YARDS RELAY
4 × 440 METRES RELAY (1749.7 yards)

U.S. CHAMPIONS 4 × 440 yards	(E. Southern, E. Young, J. Yerman, O. Davies, at Walnut, Cal., 1960.) 3 mins 5.6 secs
EMPIRE CHAMPIONS 4 × 440 yards	South Africa (Day, Evans, Spence, Potgieter) 3 mins 8.1 sec
EUROPEAN CHAMPIONS 4 × 400 Metres	Great Britain (Sampson, MacIsaac, Wrighton, Salisbury) 3 mins 7.9 secs
OLYMPIC CHAMPIONS 4 × 400 Metres	U.S.A. (Yerman, Young, G. Davis, O. Davis) 3 mins 2.2 secs

(Approximate time differential between 1600 metres and 1 mile is 1.2 secs.)

This event was first introduced to the Olympic programme in 1912, and with only three exceptions, remained an American monopoly to the present day. A British team, R. A. Lindsay, C. R. Griffiths, J. C. Ainsworth-Davis, and Guy Butler, won gold medals at Antwerp in 1920 and amassed a total time of 3 mins 22.2 secs. The world record, held exclusively by Americans in these early years, reached an impressive 3 mins 8.2 secs at Los Angeles in 1932, when a quartet including the individual 400 metres winner, Bill Carr, averaged 47.05 secs.

Great Britain scored another victory at Berlin in 1936 through the magnificent efforts of Godfrey Brown, Godfrey Rampling, Bill Roberts, and Freddie Wolff, who combined to record 3 mins 9.0 secs. This was just outside the world and Olympic record, but stood for many years as a European record. A third breach in the American monopoly occurred at Helsinki in 1952. The same Jamaican team which four years earlier had been robbed of gold medal hopes when Arthur Wint broke down on the third leg of the Wembley final, brought off a sensational victory in 3 mins 3.9 secs. The team, Les Laing, Arthur Wint, George Rhoden and Herb McKenley are the only non-American team ever to have held the world record for this event.

Great Britain were in the medals again with a third place showing at Melbourne in 1956, with 3 mins 7.2 secs by John Salisbury, Mike Wheeler, Peter Higgins, and Derek Johnson. The American winners, Charles Jenkins, Louis Jones, J. W. Mashburn, and Tom Courtney were able to total 3 mins 4.8 secs, a great performance but still shy of the Helsinki record. It fell to another great American team to eclipse the Jamaican mark at Rome with 3 mins 2.2 secs, an average of 45.5 secs each. The Germans were only half a second behind, while the current Jamaican team finished an unsung third with 3 mins 4.0 secs, or 46.0 secs per head.

Training for the 4 × 440 yards relay does not present any great technical problems. The takeover question is simpler because the incoming runner is not moving at full speed. This makes a blind baton change unnecessary, so it is in order for the receiver to look over his shoulder to make sure that he holds the baton.

Normal procedure is for the runners to race in lanes for the first leg only, but the draw for lanes is maintained at each takeover. This can be varied when two or more runners are finishing together where a last minute switch might cause a collision. It is always wise to have a team official or coach near the line to direct runners if such a disaster seems imminent.

It is often difficult for a club or school to field four good quarter-milers. In this case the side can be made up with 220- or 880-yard men and there is no doubt that either will benefit from occasional runs outside their distance. The team should try to get together at least once a fortnight for training, and while a full-course rehearsal is not necessary here, the element of team spirit is always stronger among men who have trained together. The finest example of this spirit was shown by the Jamaican team who failed at Wembley in 1952 through the breakdown of one member, but came again four years later to vindicate themselves at Helsinki.

Since participation in the relay will often constitute a double for members of the team, they should acquaint themselves with the timetable before the day. If the intervals are likely to make recovery difficult for anybody, reserves should be entered and asked to stand by.

PART TWO

Hurdling

HURDLING is a refinement of sprinting, a technique of adapting fast running to the pattern imposed by a predictable course of obstacles. A hurdler must in fact be a sprinter with a grasp of the principles of running outlined in Part One together with the qualities of suppleness and timing, co-ordinated in fluent hurdle clearance which it is the purpose of this section to describe.

Development of technique: the earliest hurdle races, in about 1840, were simply run-and-jump affairs, but by 1860 a technique had been evolved in which the leading leg was sliced diagonally across the hurdle allowing the seat to pass closer to the bar than in an ordinary jump. The modern style of using a straight leading leg probably originated in about 1886 at Oxford University. Up till that time hurdles were planted in the ground which did not encourage the kind of recklessness which makes for fast times. The modern hurdle is required by the rules to have a toppling moment of eight pounds, but the athlete who crashes is not, like his hurdling ancestors, destined for severe injury, particularly if his style is correct.

Hurdle exercises: it is obvious from the action pictures (facing page 128) that hurdle action requires an exceptional degree of suppleness. The hurdler must therefore perform exercises to prepare his muscles for these rather unnatural movements, and should never attempt to hurdle without having first warmed-up carefully, not only with jogging, striding and exercises.

The following exercises are good value for hurdling: leg

43

swinging from the hip both longitudinally and laterally while holding on to a bar (Fig. 9); trunk turning and twisting with feet apart; ground hurdling (Fig. 8). These exercises should occupy at least ten minutes of gradual and repeated

Figure 8

movement. They should be carried out before every training session and competition, and also on rest days if possible. Time spent on stretching exercises will repay the hurdler tenfold; they are an insurance against injury and a passport to efficient hurdling.

Hurdle clearance: having warmed-up thoroughly there is no exercise for the hurdler better than hurdling. Precise details of hurdle measurement and stride planning are incorporated in the sections dealing with the three main hurdle events, but the beginner can start by practising over a low hurdle of 2 ft. 6 in. Assuming that he takes off from his right foot, although this is an individual matter, the procedure will be as follows:

Mark the track at a point about six feet from the hurdle run up at a good pace, taking off from the right foot at the mark, lifting the left knee high and thrusting the leg straight out across the hurdle. At the same time throw the right arm forward and keep the left arm at the side. The trailing leg will rotate at the hip and cross the bar at right angles to the leading leg. If the approach and take-off have been straight, the landing should be balanced, with the left foot bearing the weight and driving the body forward into the next stride.

After repeated runs over the low hurdle, a 3-ft. hurdle should be attempted. Mark a take-off point about seven feet from the hurdle. Approach as before, lead fast with the left leg and at the same time dip forward from the waist. Body dip cultivates forward rotation and helps to bring the hurdler to earth without delay. It also frees his hips for a comfortable sweep through of the trailing leg. A sore

Figure 9

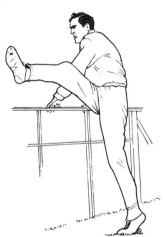

trailing ankle is nearly always due to an upright position over the hurdle.

The beginner will probably not profit by taking more than fifteen or twenty runs at a hurdle in one session. Muscles grow tired quickly in unaccustomed effort and it is better to return fresh than rehearse a technique that has become faulty from fatigue. The salient points to watch are direction, which can be checked by studying footprints, a fast leading leg, which alone can produce the split position needed between take-off and clearance, and body dip. The hurdler who runs straight at the obstacle, jack-knifes quickly, and dips low, cannot go far wrong.

120 YARDS HURDLES
110 METRES HURDLES (120.25 yards)

U.S. CHAMPION 120 YARDS   Lee Calhoun (Berne, Switzerland, 1960) 13.2 secs
EMPIRE CHAMPION 120 YARDS   Keith Gardner (Jamaica) 14.0 secs
EUROPEAN CHAMPION 110 METRES   Martin Lauer (Germany) 13.7 secs
OLYMPIC CHAMPION 110 METRES Lee Calhoun (U.S.A.) 13.8 secs
(Times for 120 yards and 110 metres are equivalent.)

In 1886 C. N. Jackson of Oxford set a best British performance for 120 yards hurdles of 16.0 secs, His name is given to a trophy awarded annually to the United Kingdom athlete responsible for the best A.A.A. Championship performance. Another Oxonian, A. C. M. Croome, achieved 15.6 secs with something approaching a modern straight leading leg action, but it fell to an American, Alva Kraenzlein, to develop this style and record 15.2 secs in 1898. An even 15.0 secs was posted by another American, Forrest Smithson, in capturing the 1908 Olympic gold medal at White City.

A giant Canadian named Earl Thomson became the first human officially to break 15.0 secs in 1920 with the surprising mark of 14.4 secs. Thomson confirmed his prowess with an Olympic title at Antwerp the same year. The first Englishman to lower the even time barrier was Lord Burghley, better known over the long hurdles, who reduced the English native record to 14.8 secs and in 1930 to an unratified but apparently fair 14.5 secs. From that date until 1950, British high hurdling was dominated by Donald Finlay who graduated from a bronze medal in the 1932 Olympics to silver in 1936. Finlay also collected the Empire and European crowns, setting a British best of 14.3 secs when winning the latter title at Paris in 1938.

Meanwhile in 1935 a unique event in track history had occurred when two Americans, Roy Staley and Phil Cope, dead-heated in 14.2 secs to equal the world record already jointly held by two other Americans. This quartet made way in 1936 for Forrest Towns with 14.1 secs. Towns became Olympic Champion at Berlin and a month later was timed at an astounding 13.7 secs at Oslo for a niche in history that was undisturbed until 1948.

In that year the dapper Harrison Dillard ran 13.6 secs but was eliminated in the U.S. Olympic tryouts and qualified for the Wembley 100 metres to win the final. Dillard then qualified for the 1952 Olympic 100 metres hurdles and set the seal on a fabulous career with another gold medal.

Jack Davis, a burly Californian who had lost to Dillard at Helsinki but shared his Olympic record of 13.7 secs, clipped the world record to 13.4 secs, but was again deprived of gold medal honours in 1956. It was Lee Calhoun who gained an inches decision in the Melbourne final with 13.5 secs, a time again shared by Davis. In 1959 Germany's Martin Lauer lowered the world record to the improbable level of 13.2 secs on the superbly fast Zürich track. This mark was equalled in 1960 by Lee Calhoun, who confirmed his supremacy by retaining his Olympic title at Rome.

In the past, successful high hurdlers were often moderate sprinters with the height and mobility to master good hurdle technique. Today the pace of hurdling ensures that only first-class sprinters can win, so speed must be combined with height as the necessary physical qualities of the top class high hurdler. Lee Calhoun and Martin Lauer are both 6 ft. 1 in. tall, the former capable of 9.6 secs for 100 yards, the latter a member of the winning Olympic 4 × 100 metres relay team at Rome. Two notable exceptions to the tall man axiom are Keith Gardner (5 ft. 8 in.) and Harrison Dillard (5 ft. 10 in.), but both made up with exceptional speed, Gardner being the reigning Empire Games 100 yards Champion and Dillard the 1948 Olympic sprint Champion as already mentioned.

Measurements: in the 120 yards hurdles the approach to the first hurdle is 15 yards, the ten 3 ft. 6 in. hurdles are spaced at 10-yard intervals, and the run in from the last hurdle is 15 yards.

Stride planning: the art and science of good hurdling consists as much in synchronizing running strides with the hurdle spacings as in clearing the obstacles. The great majority of high hurdlers take eight strides to the first hurdle. This entails a right foot forward starting position for a right foot take-off and vice versa. A few tall men take seven strides to the first hurdle, and in this case the alternate foot would be in front in the starting position. It is imperative that the correct position be established from the outset and adhered to in all races because it is the first detail in a continuous pattern of precision. Three strides are always taken between hurdles bringing the same foot down at the take-off to each hurdle.

Training for form: given the preliminary work on hurdle form outlined on page 44, the high hurdler should always practise with a 3 ft. 6 in. hurdle from a 15-yard approach. Having warmed-up, he should first do starts with one hurdle, concentrating on reaching the take-off mark in an even stride progression. The only way to achieve this is by trial and error, using the thought impression left by each attempt as a guide to adjustment in the next run. Since both mind and body can only assimilate technique in small doses, it is best to break away after three or four runs and return after a rest or a stride along the straight with the sprinters.

As soon as confidence is gained with one hurdle, training with two or more hurdles should go forward. The difficulty experienced by many beginners in reaching three strides between hurdles is due to lack of impetus caused either by flat-footedness or unbalance. These flaws should not exist if the basic elements of direction, fast leading leg, and body dip have been applied. With these present, the initial impetus of the run up should carry across the first hurdle and through to the second and succeeding hurdles. Again the thought impression of each attempt should suggest adjustment and three or four consecutive runs are generally enough. Then a break for rest or change of activity will renew capacity for full concentration on another group of three or four starts.

As with any complex sequence of physical movement, typing is an obvious example, the components of good hurdling can only be perfected by assiduous repetition which gradually wears smooth the paths of nervous impulse and muscular co-ordination until the routine becomes automatic. Ultimately the best training is a full-flight rehearsal, demanding concentration for the duration of a race and bringing perfective polish to bear on every link in the chain of synchronized action.

Since hurdling is sprinting, training for condition should

follow the lines of the programme suggested for the 100-yard man, with work on hurdling technique thrown in. In Month 2 the training should become more specialized with the emphasis on grooving speed into the hurdle spacings.

Month 1

Training programme for one week.

1st day. Free running 30 minutes, including stretches of striding up to 150 yards.

2nd day. Track. 15–20 minutes practice over one hurdle for form. 6 × 60 yards or 4 × 150 yards intervals with sprinters.

3rd day. Track. Practice over one hurdle. 2 sets of 3 starts over two or three hurdles with a short rest between sets. A fast striding 220 with sprinters.

4th day. Hill running session with sprinters.

5th day. Weight or circuit training combined with hurdle exercises. Alternatively free running.

Month 2

Training programme for one week.

1st day. Track. Practice over one hurdle. 3 sets of 3 starts over two or three hurdles in company, resting between sets. Time trial over 120 yards flat.

2nd day. Practice over one hurdle. One or two good starts over two hurdles. Repetition work or starts with sprinters.

3rd day. Two or three time trials over 60 yards and five hurdles, i.e. half the full 120-yard course. Rest between efforts and note times as a guide to the amount of exercise which produces the optimum warm-up.

4th day. More work on short starts over hurdles. Finish with a fast run over 150–200 yards. Jogging.

5th day. Weight or circuit training.

When competition begins, the kind of training needed to maintain fitness should follow the lines of second and third days in Month 2.

220 YARDS HURDLES
200 METRES HURDLES (218.72 yards)

U.S. CHAMPION 220 YARDS   Donald A. Styron (Baton Rouge, La., 1960) 21.9 secs

This event does not figure in major championship competition.

(Approximate time differential between 200 metres and 220 yards is 0.1 secs.)

The low hurdles originated in the United States so it was perhaps natural that Americans should have taken the gold medals on the two occasions, 1900 and 1904, that it was included in the Olympic programme. Alva Kraenzlein and Harry Hillman were the respective victors, each recording 25.4 secs. Kraenzlein had set a world record of 23.6 secs in 1898 to add to his honours in the 'highs'.

Another American monopoly, the world low hurdle records until recent times were all set on straight tracks and the first human officially to better 23.0 secs was the versatile Jesse Owens. Since the 'lows' was only a sideline, his 220-yards hurdles record mark of 22.6 secs was destined for a shorter life than the sprint and long jump records which he set on the same afternoon in 1935. Five years later, Fred Wolcott, a joint holder with Forrest Towns of the high hurdle record, turned in a time of 22.5 secs and was credited with 22.3 secs at the 200-metre line.

Lord Burghley was the pioneer of English low hurdling

of under 25.0 secs class when he clocked 24.8 secs in 1925. Burghley improved the official native record to 24.6 secs and it is estimated that he achieved 24.3 secs when losing a duel with a Cambridge contemporary, Bob Tisdall, by one yard in 1930. Twenty years elapsed before another Light Blue, Simon Brooks, clipped the mark to an even 24.0 secs. After a similar interval Paul Vine, a Dark Blue, broke through with 23.7 secs in winning the A.A.A. title in 1955, this time being equalled in 1961 by Mike Parker of Cambridge.

The world list meanwhile had undergone dramatic revision with Harrison Dillard racing to 22.3 secs on a half-turn at Salt Lake City in 1947. Dave Sime, a pure sprinter, was responsible for a tenth reduction in 1956, but like Owens was more concerned with sprint records and his hurdle mark survived just two years until the coloured Elias Gilbert posted 22.1 secs. A time barrier which many runners would be proud to break on the flat was shattered in 1960 when America's Don Styron recorded an epic 21.9 secs.

Following the I.A.A.F.'s decision to recognize 220 yards and 200 metres records set on a turn, Germany's Martin Lauer recorded a separately listed mark for 200 metres hurdles of 22.5 secs in 1959. This was equalled by Glenn Davis in 1960 three weeks before successfully defending his Olympic 400 metres title at Rome.

Measurements: in the 220 yards hurdles there are ten 2 ft. 6 in. hurdles spaced at 20-yard intervals, with a 20-yard run-up to the first and a 20-yard run-in from the last hurdle.

Stride planning: it is usual to take ten strides to the first hurdle, thus a right-foot-forward starting position would lead to a right-foot take-off and vice versa. As in the high hurdles, it is possible to lead with either foot, but left-foot leaders are at an advantage because it is easier for them to hurdle on an anti-clockwise turn. Hurdlers who lead with the right leg lose ground by having to run in the middle of their lane so that their trailing leg passes over the hurdle and not inside it in contravention of the rules. Seven strides are taken between hurdles and since this is a long stride, the hurdler must be well on his toes and make full use of his arms if he is to reach his next hurdle within take-off range.

Technique: the low hurdler does not need to bound much to clear his obstacles and consequently need not alter the running angle of his body when hurdling. A slight forward dip at each hurdle will assist rotation into the next stride, but the exaggerated lean of high hurdling is not necessary.

Special training for the 'lows'

Most low hurdlers combine the event with their speciality which may be sprinting, high hurdling or quarter-mile hurdling. If this is so, the occasional time trial over half the course on the turn is a useful workout. For those who wish to make the 'lows' their speciality the following sample week of training is offered:

1st day. Several starts over two low hurdles on the turn, concentrating on holding the line. One or two fast striding runs over 250–300 yards.

2nd day. Starts with the sprinters. Two good time-trials over 110 yards and five low hurdles on the turn, as for a race.

3rd day. Starts with sprinters. Two three-quarter speed runs over the full 200 yards course with hurdles, concentrating on holding form over the last few hurdles.

4th day. Training with quarter-milers.

5th day. Weight or circuit training.

The heavy emphasis on stamina training is due to the need to develop the strength to hold the same stride pattern at the end of a hard 220 as at the beginning. Experience will show that this is the hardest aspect of the low hurdle event. Since, in fact, it is impossible to keep an even stride length the whole way, it is probably best to compromise by taking the first hurdles as snappily as possible while the legs are fresh and seven strides fitting comfortably into the spacings. Then as striding becomes more difficult it will help to take a longer hurdle clearance, leaving a slightly shorter distance to cover in seven strides. The full flight training suggested will help to give the hurdler the feel of these adjustments.

440 YARDS HURDLES
400 METRES HURDLES (437.44 yards)

U.S. CHAMPION 440 YARDS   Glenn Davis (at Bakersfield, Cal., 1958)   49.9 secs
EMPIRE CHAMPION 440 YARDS   Gert Potgieter (S.A.)
49.7 secs
EUROPEAN CHAMPION 400 METRES   Yuriy Lituyev
(U.S.S.R.) 51.1 secs
OLYMPIC CHAMPION 400 METRES Glenn Davis (U.S.A.)
49.3 secs

(Approximate time differential 400 metres and 440 yards is 0.3 secs)

One of the earliest hurdlers rash enough to test his powers over 440 yards was G. B. Shaw, a New Zealander resident in England, who set a world's best of 57.2 secs in 1891. This mark was not approached by the first Olympic gold medallist, America's Walter Tewkesbury in 1900, and stood until another Englishman, G. R. L. Anderson, ran 56.8 secs in 1910. The introduction of the 440 hurdles to both English and American championships in 1914 paved the way for progress. However it was not until 1920 that the record was lowered to a respectable 54.2 secs by John Norton, but only a month later he was beaten by a fellow-American, Frank Loomis, in the Olympic final with a metric world record of 54.0 secs at Antwerp.

In 1924 F. Morgan Taylor became Olympic champion in 52.6 secs but this was not accepted as a world record under the rules then in force, because he overturned one hurdle. Norton's old linear record of 54.2 secs was the target of the up-and-coming Lord Burghley's efforts, and on the 2nd July 1927 he exactly equalled this mark only to find that it had been beaten in America by John Gibson, who, within hours of Burghley's performance had reached a new level of 52.6 secs. Burghley lived up to the American challenge at the Amsterdam Olympics in 1928 when he toured the fifth lane with fierce determination to win in 53.4 secs. Another Cambridge blue to become gold medallist at the next Games in Los Angeles, was the Irishman Bob Tisdall. His winning 51.8 secs was well inside Morgan Taylor's 1927 world record but was unacceptable again due to an upset hurdle. Tisdall however had the satisfaction of defeating both Taylor and Burghley, running in their third Olympiad.

A new era in 400 metres hurdling was initiated by the famous Glenn 'Slats' Hardin who took the world's best to an incredible 50.6 secs in 1934 and improved his Los Angeles silver medal rating to gold in the Berlin Olympic final in 1936. Hardin's record endured the onslaughts of the first two post-war Olympic champions, Roy Cochran and Charlie Moore, the latter reaching 50.8 secs for 400 metres and a relatively modest linear 51.6 secs at White City in

1952. It took Soviet Russia's Yuriy Lituyev to remove both Hardin's and Moore's records with times of 50.4 secs and 51.3 secs. Lituyev was eclipsed in his second Olympic final at Melbourne in 1956 by the rugged Glenn Davis who had already proclaimed his metal by slicing the Russian's world 400 metres record to 49.5 secs.

In 1957 South Africa's Gert Potgieter laid claim to a share of Davis's prowess with a 440 yards world record of 50.7 secs on grass. Within a year the answer to this was found, first by the coloured American, Josh Culbreath, and then by Davis himself in 49.9 secs. Undismayed, Potgieter replied with 49.7 secs in winning the Empire title and in 1960 with 49.3 secs. Since this was relatively faster than Glenn Davis's metric record of 49.2 secs set at Budapest in 1958, the prospect of an Olympic duel between the pair at Rome was intriguing. Potgieter was however severely injured in a motor accident which ruined his Olympic hopes and allowed Davis to retain his title at Rome.

In Britain Lord Burghley's native 440-yard record of 53.8 secs was nineteen years old when Harry Whittle first reduced it by a tenth in 1949. Whittle improved to 52.7 secs but was unable to match the peer's metric best of 52.2 secs which survived as a reminder of the Los Angeles Olympic final until 1954. In that year Harry Kane became the tenant of both British records when running a game second to the world record breaking Lituyev with times of 51.5 secs and 51.8 secs in the same race. In 1958, Chris Goudge recorded a place time of 51.6 secs for 440 yards, while Tom Farrell posted superlative international wins over the Russians in 1957 (51.1 secs) and the Italians in 1960 (51·0 secs) to annex the United Kingdom 400 metres hurdles record.

Measurements: there are ten 3 ft. hurdles spaced 38¼ yards apart with an approach to the first hurdle of 49¼ yards and a run in from the last hurdle of 46½ yards.

Stride planning: it is usual to take 22 strides to the first hurdle which, being an even number, will call for the same foot being in front at the start as is being used for take-off at the first hurdle. Most hurdlers take fifteen strides between hurdles, reverting to seventeen strides in the last few gaps where fatigue makes it impossible to hold the fifteen stride rhythm. A two-stride increase is necessary because few hurdlers can hurdle off either foot and seventeen strides will ensure take-off from the same foot.

After experiment with the approach and stride pattern between the first two hurdles, the beginner should give careful thought to the question of stride planning over the full distance. It will be obvious that in a race where fatigue is a definite factor, stride precision cannot be achieved to the same degree as in the shorter events. Furthermore, as the hurdles are spaced more widely, the margin for error and variation in length of stride is much greater. Even the existence of a moderate wind along the track can drastically affect the hurdler's attempts to synchronize his strides with the spacings.

A few hurdlers have devised alternatives to the orthodox fifteen stride pattern to suit their individual needs and these may supply a useful guide to experiment by the 440 hurdles aspirant. Lituyev, a tall, long-striding athlete, used to run thirteen strides between the first eight gaps and fourteen in the last two. This meant clearing the ninth hurdle off the wrong foot, and Lituyev went to great pains to rehearse this because he knew it was more economical to distribute his effort in that way than to make the bigger adjustment to fifteen strides in the last two gaps. The fifteen-stride hurdler could well consider taking sixteen strides in the last two gaps rather than dropping back to seventeen, which, however tired he may be, will restrict him severely. An even more flexible method was used by Potgieter who was equally efficient at hurdling off either foot which meant that he did not need consciously to adjust his strides but simply ran and hurdled all the way with uninhibited flow. Glenn Davis used fifteen strides all the way, but definitely appeared at Rome to be over-striding in the early gaps of the Olympic final, showing that his running power was not being utilized to the best advantage within the hurdle spacings.

Special training: clearly the quarter-mile hurdler must be a good quarter-miler and it is not necessary to repeat the training outlined for the 440 yards which he should carry out. His main problem is to harness his 440 fitness to the hurdle course so, much of his repetition work must be devoted to acquiring judgement of stride length and pace. A race run at even pace will be one in which stride planning is most likely to be efficient, and it is quite possible that the hurdler will enhance his ability on the flat by this very attention to pace distribution.

As in the other hurdle events, the last three hurdles are the stage in which most can go wrong and therefore the aspect of the race in which rehearsal is most profitable. Full flight runs in practice are therefore imperative. Experience will enable him to estimate his chances of reaching the next hurdle in his chosen stride pattern from the previous hurdle, so that he can decide to adjust immediately, obviating the fatal shuffle which results from a late change of plan.

Occasional competitions on the flat will give an indication of progress in these skills by providing a comparison with times achieved over hurdles. A good differential is three seconds. Most athletes will benefit from some experience of all three hurdle events but the best results are ultimately the outcome of specialization because that is the only way to become completely attuned to a particular hurdle routine.

PART THREE

Middle and long distance running

THE half-mile is the shortest track distance which cannot be described as a sprint so it can conveniently be linked with the remaining track events up to 6 miles, and the 3,000 metres steeplechase in a section devoted to middle and long distances.

That methods of training for all these events have a great deal in common can be judged from the fact that certain athletes have been able to hold records at a wide range of distances. In the twenties Paavo Nurmi, the 'Flying Finn', held world records from 1500 metres to 1 hour (in which he covered 11 miles 1,648 yards). During the war, Gunder Hägg led the world from 1500 to 5000 metres, while in more recent history, Sandor Iharos of Hungary held most of the linear and metric marks from 1500 to 10,000 metres simultaneously. This was possible because the range of pace encountered in these events, 15 m.p.h. in the mile to nearly 13 m.p.h. at six miles, and 12 miles run in a full hour, is not great. The same kind of ability is required, and given an adequate background of conditioning, any runner should be able to attempt all these distances without difficulty.

It is therefore important to accept that the approach to middle-distance running need not be too specialized from the outset. A runner is unlikely to reach full maturity without experience of a range of distances; having then decided which event suits his natural rhythm best, he will achieve the best results by specializing.

In training for the middle distances, perhaps more than any other department of athletics, the old truth that there is no substitute for hard work is relevant. The kind of distances which great runners cover, often between 50 and 100 miles a week in training, is the plainest indication of what is required. A man who has done so much running cannot help but acquire an economical action, good muscular condition appropriate to his task, and a familiarity with the symptoms of fatigue amounting almost to disregard. But though running and plenty of it is the basis of the answer to middle-distance training, history has produced certain formal and informal methods of conditioning which most runners include in their preparation. These methods fall into three main categories, free running, interval running, and resistance training for strength.

Free running: most authorities are agreed that this is the fundamental and most important aspect of middle-distance training. The Swedish word 'fartlek', meaning speed-play, is often used to describe this form of exercise. As the name implies, it involves running at will, fast and slow, without any set limits or indeed in any particular surroundings. The runner merely sets out. and conscious neither of the distance covered nor the time taken, indulges in the simple luxury of movement.

Free running formed the basis of middle-distance training among the great Finnish and Swedish runners of the Paavo Nurmi and Gunder Hägg eras, and today is emphatically recommended both by Percy Cerutty, coach to Herb Elliott, and by Arthur Lydiard, coach to the two Olympic champions from New Zealand, Peter Snell (800 metres) and Murray Halberg (5,000 metres), among other experts.

The free running included in sprint training schedules differs from this only in so far as the sprinter does not wish to spend too much time on easy pace running because he is too busy learning how to sprint. The middle-distance man, by contrast, cannot do too much of it. Since he will undoubtedly be covering a good mileage, it is wise to select grass in preference to harder surfaces for free running. Many Continental training centres have sawdust paths which are ideally resilient. The runner should also invest in a pair of shoes with sponge-rubber insoles to help offset the tendency to muscle soreness in the lower leg which heavy mileage produces. It is also important to vary the course taken to avoid any tendency to become formalized and repetitive.

A typical free-running outing might take the runner from 5 to 15 miles, and with stretches of medium-fast running, and occasional bursts of sprinting, might occupy anything from 30 to 90 minutes, according to the track distance for which he is training.

Interval running consists of repeated runs over a pre-determined distance interspersed with stretches of easy running for recovery. The interval unit is usually an even distance such as 220, 440 or 660 yards, which can be con-veniently related in time to the pace of the runner's chosen event. Thus a miler capable of 4 mins. 20 secs, who would ideally run his race in four even laps of 65 secs, might well start his interval training with laps of 68 or 70 secs, inter-spersed with laps of jogging taking perhaps 3 mins each. A good workout would involve between five and ten such intervals, with the same number of slow laps for recovery. As fitness develops he can reduce the unit time to below his racing pace of 65 secs and also reduce the recovery time The system is, of course, capable of infinite variation.

This kind of training not only gives him a useful drill in pace judgement, but also builds his stamina in gradual stages by spreading the onset of fatigue over a longer period than would obtain in a race. In this way he can get more value out of training by digging deeper, as it were, into his reserves, and if he has a good background of free running, the benefit from interval training will be correspondingly greater.

Most middle-distance runners carry out interval training at some stage in their preparation, some using it almost exclusively. The pupils of Mihaily Igloi, the famous Hungarian coach, including Iharos, Rozsavölgyi and other Hungarian and American record holders, have been devotees of intervals. The training schedules of Franz Stampfl, who advised Bannister, Chataway, and Brasher, also show a marked preference for this form of preparation.

The only shortcoming of interval training is that when carried to the extreme, it can make the runner too clock conscious. Though admirable as a means of grooving a running rhythm close to racing speed, it can also give him too accurate a knowledge of his own limitations. Ideally it should be treated as complementary to free running in the middle-distance training programme, one being less effective without the other.

Subsidiary training for strength: though the runner is more concerned with economy and endurance in the middle distances, he should not lose sight of the necessity of getting stronger in the muscular sense. Weight and circuit training under experienced supervision can be performed with benefit by all runners, though indiscriminate indulgence may be harmful. Another excellent form of resistance training is uphill running. This is also carried out by a great many top-class runners, notably those who attend Percy Cerutty's training camp at Portsea in Australia, where the sand dunes present a natural course for uphill running.

In effect, uphill running is a variant of interval training, because recovery intervals at a slower speed are needed between climbs. The increased resistance met in hill-climbing is an excellent method of building leg-power, and as a means of inducing fatigue and bringing the runner face-to-face with the most painful effects of hard exercise, this form of training is without equal. However, since it involves a rather over-accentuated knee-lift, it is probably best confined to the preliminary training period and left alone during the competitive season.

Cross-country running in the competitive sense is no longer regarded by experts as a training method for middle distances. It is really a speciality in its own right, involving a tough and prolonged season which cannot effectively be combined with a full track season. Nevertheless cross-country brings rewards and good-fellowship which its devotees rate higher than those of track athletics, and many are prepared to sacrifice their chances in the latter for the rigours of the 'rough'.

The general indications on middle-distance training outlined in this introduction are relevant to all the events dealt with more specifically in the ensuing pages. The training schedules should be used as a guide only. The suggested alternatives in interval running for example, are capable of infinite variation, and the runner should increase the volume of his work as his capacity grows. In the long process of building himself up physically he will also become mentally hardened to the hardships of the toughest competitive sport there is. This psychological preparation is perhaps best summed up in the words of a famous coach who told his charge 'keep going son, to feel tired is not to be tired'.

In addition to training methods, there are competitive aspects of middle-distance running which can be regarded as pertaining to all the events dealt with in Part Three.

Above: Olympic 100 metres final, Rome, 1960; left to right: Armin Hary (Germany) first, Peter Radford (G.B.) third, Enrique Figuerola (Cuba) fourth, Ray Norton (U.S.A.) sixth, hidden—Frank Budd (U.S.A.) fifth, Dave Sime (U.S.A.) second. Time 10·2 secs., Olympic record. *Below:* Olympic 200 metres final, Rome, 1960; left to right: Stone Johnson (U.S.A.) fifth, hidden—Marian Foik (Poland) fourth, Abdoulaye Seye (France) third, Lester Carney (U.S.A.) second, Livio Berruti (Italy) first. Time 20·5 secs., Olympic and world record.

Above: First semi-final, Olympic 400 metres, Rome, 1960; left to right: Manfred Kinder (Germany) third, Robbie Brightwell (G.B.) fourth, Milka Singh (India) second, Otis Davis (U.S.A.) first. Time 45·5 secs., Olympic record. *Below:* Second semi-final, Olympic 400 metres, Rome, 1960; left to right: Abdul Amu (Nigeria) fourth, Earl Young (U.S.A.) third, Mal Spence (S.A.) second, Carl Kaufmann (Germany) first. Both Davis, the winner, and Kaufmann, set a new Olympic and world record of 44·9 secs. in the final.

Above: Olympic 4 × 100 metres relay final, Rome, 1960; Great Britain on their way to bronze medals: Peter Radford hands over to Nick Whitehead. *Below:* Olympic 4 × 400 metres relay second semi-final, Rome 1960; Glenn Davis (U.S.A.) hands over to Otis Davis; George Kerr (West Indies) has just received from Mal Spence, on the ground.

Left: 4 × 880 yards relay world record attempt, White City, 1960: Peter Snell (N.Z.), the Olympic 800 metres champion, finishes the anchor leg. The time of 7 mins. 18·0 secs. was inside the official record but could not be accepted as the team, Snell, Tony Blue (Australia), George Kerr (West Indies) and Tom Farrell (G.B.), was a mixed one. *Right:* White City, 1958: the fastest mile ever run in Britain. Herb Elliott (Australia) leads Brian Hewson (G.B.). Times 3 mins. 55·4 secs. and 3 mins. 58·9 secs.

Above: Germany v. U.S.S.R. match, Augsburg, 1958; left to right: Martin Lauer (Germany) beats Anatoliy Mikhailov (U.S.S.R.) in the 110 metres hurdles in 13·8 secs. *Below:* Olympic 400 metres hurdles final, Rome, 1960: Glenn Davis (U.S.A.) takes the last hurdle. His winning time, 49·3 secs., Olympic record.

Above: England v. Russian F.R., White City, 1961: Valeriy Brumel (U.S.S.R.), who at the age of twenty raised the world record to 7 ft. 4½ ins. *Below:* Olympic high jump final, Rome, 1960: Robert Shavlakadze (U.S.S.R.) wins with a straddle of 7 ft. 1 in.

Above and below: Flight and landing: Ralph Boston (U.S.A.), Olympic long jump champion, 1960, who set a world record of 27 ft. 2 ins. in 1961.

Left: Don Bragg (U.S.A.), Olympic pole vault champion, 1960, in action at White City. *Right:* Great Britain v. U.S.A. match, White City, 1961: Henry Wadsworth (U.S.A.) sets a United Kingdom all-comers pole vault record of 15 ft. 2 ins.

Tactics are the middle-distance man's skills in making the fullest use of his physical and mental resources in beating his opponents. Broadly speaking they can be divided into two interdependent factors, pace judgement and positioning.

Pace Judgement: it is generally accepted that even pace running is the most economical way of distributing effort in endurance events. This knowledge is based not only on the cumulative experience of runners for over fifty years, but also on scientific experiment. Tables showing the intermediate lap times registered in record-breaking performances from 880 yards to six miles have been compiled as a guide to pace judgement. It will be noted that perfect even pace running does not actually obtain in practice. This is because the even pace principle, though certainly the best way of achieving fast time, must always be qualified by the primary objective of a race which is winning. It would clearly be unwise to run an even pace to the extent of getting out of touch with the opposition. Here the runner must consider the vital importance in middle distance of positioning.

Positioning: the golden rule is 'follow rather than lead'. For physical and psychological reasons it is easier to stride comfortably in another man's wake than to bear the burden of pace making. Thus unless the pace is absurdly fast, it is wisest to keep with the leaders and reserve any attempt at leading for the finish. It may sometimes be necessary to overtake at an earlier stage if it is known that a particular rival has a faster finish. In this case it might be effective to break away and draw his sting by a long sustained burst. A few exceptional runners are able to win after leading all or most of the way, but such men are rare. In general the front runner is not a winner.

Another aspect of positioning is avoidance of body

contact and of getting boxed in. There is generally some jostling on the first turn of a middle-distance race when the field converges on the curb. The runner should be alert for known offenders and depend on a vigorous arm action to maintain his balance until the field has spread out. The best way to avoid getting boxed in is to run at the shoulder of the man in front, that is about two feet from the curb. In this way he can overtake with the minimum delay when necessary, and also curtail the freedom of other runners to overtake him on the outside. He can always move in near the curb when rounding a turn to avoid running over his distance, and then move out again in the straight to secure his escape route at his opponent's shoulder. Here too he will be out of danger from the trailing spikes of the man in front.

The importance of good positioning becomes even more apparent in the later stages of a race, when fatigue makes it increasingly difficult to recover from the effects of jostling, or to escape from a box. Assuming that the runner has succeeded in keeping in touch with the leaders until the last lap, he must concentrate on preserving his position and his form with the object of challenging as late as possible. The golden rule that it is easier to follow than to lead is never more applicable than in the finishing straight, where a fading runner is most vulnerable in the eyes of those behind him. Many big races have been lost by runners who challenged too early and presented sitting targets for strong-finishing rivals in the closing strides. The most obvious but most neglected axiom of middle-distance tactics is that it is essential to lead at only one stage in a race—at the tape.

On the day of competition: the following general guidance for all middle-distance runners may be useful. Arrange to be at the track at least one hour before you are due to race. Report to the competitor's steward, collect your number, pin it on your vest, ascertain your heat number and qualifying conditions (if this applies to your distance) and make sure that you have no other distractions for 45 minutes before you run. Having warmed-up go to the start with 10 minutes to spare, complete with starting blocks if you are using them.

If you have to compete in a final on the same day, rest on your back in the dressing room and return to the track with 10 minutes to spare for the final. Under the rules at least 50 minutes rest is allowed between heat and final of a half-mile, and in the case of a mile, one hour, though milers are seldom called on to run more than once in a day.

After the race make an immediate post-mortem with the help of friends and onlookers and note intermediate lap times carefully as a guide to future efforts.

880 YARDS   800 METRES (874.9 yards)

U.S. CHAMPION 880 YARDS	Thomas Courtney (at L.A., 1957) 1 min 46.8 secs
EMPIRE CHAMPION 880 YARDS	Herb Elliott(Australia) 1 min 49.3 secs
EUROPEAN CHAMPION 800 METRES	Mike Rawson(G.B.) 1 min 47.8 secs
OLYMPIC CHAMPION 800 METRES	Peter Snell (N.Z.) 1 min 46.3 secs

(Approximate time differential between 800 metres and 880 yards is 0.7 secs.)

Lawrence Myers, whose role in one-lap history has already been mentioned, also recorded a world's best of 1 min 55.4 secs for 880 yards in 1884. After four years, a burly

Oxonian named F. J. K. Cross trimmed exactly a second from this mark but relinquished the summit in 1895 to another American, Charlie Kilpatrick, with 1 min 53.4 secs. The achievements of the great Ted Meredith included an Olympic title for America in 1912 and world records for 800 metres in 1 min 51.9 secs, and 880 yards in 1 min 52.5 secs, timed at both points in the Stockholm Olympic final.

British runners, following the example of Alfred Tysoe in 1900, took gold medals in four successive Olympiads. Albert Hill collected an 800 and 1500 metres double in 1920, while Douglas Lowe was victorious with strategic performances in 1924 and 1928, lowering Meredith's Olympic record to 1 min 51.8 secs in retaining his title. In 1932, Tom Hampson treated the Los Angeles crowds to an impeccable display of pace judgement to set a world record of 1 min 49.8 secs. Meredith's half-mile record yielded in 1926 to Germany's Otto Peltzer who, in posting a time of 1 min 51.6 secs, inflicted a rare defeat on Lowe.

Ben Eastman, of quarter-mile fame, next led the world at 880 yards with 1 min 49.8 secs, which for want of metric timekeepers could only be listed as equalling Hampson's 800 metres time. In 1938 a specially paced event at Motspur Park in Surrey was the occasion of the immortal Sydney Wooderson's arrival in the world record books with times of 1 min 48.4 secs for 800 metres and 1 min 49.2 secs for 880 yards in the same race.

Sensational though these times seemed, they were eclipsed within a year by Germany's Rudolph Harbig with an astounding 1 min 46.6 secs 800 metres run at Milan. A month later he set a 400 metres record of 46.0 secs and in 1941 added the 1000 metres best to his honours. Since 880 yards timekeepers had not been on hand to provide evidence of Harbig's obvious ability to beat the 880 yards record, this stood until 1954 when Denmark's Gunnar Nielsen, of four-minute fame, produced 1 min 48.6 secs. A powerful American negro, Mal Whitfield, who matched Lowe's achievement by retaining his 1948 Wembley 800 metres title at Helsinki in 1952, also displayed remarkable consistency in clocking 1 min 49.2 secs on each occasion.

Harbig's phenomenal 800 metres record finally cracked under the assault of Roger Moens the Belgian policeman, in 1955. Moens was timed in 1 min 45.7 secs, while Audun Boysen gave his compatriots at Bislet Stadium in Oslo an added thrill by pursuing him in 1 min 45.9 secs. Tom Courtney, the 1956 Olympic champion, set an 880 yards record of 1 min 46.8 secs at Los Angeles in 1956, but failed by a tenth to equal Moens's metric mark.

Wooderson's time stood as a United Kingdom best until 1955 when it passed alternately to Derek Johnson and Brian Hewson, the latter having the last say in 1958 with 1 min 47.8 secs. Johnson, who had only narrowly conceded the Olympic gold medal to Courtney at Melbourne, took the United Kingdom 800 metres best to 1 min 46.6 secs at Oslo in 1957. Roger Moens, who had missed the Melbourne Games through injury, was ousted from long-awaited gold medal honours at Rome by the rugged Peter Snell, but five years after his heyday, recorded a most worthy 1 min 46.5 secs in second place.

The half-mile is probably the most comprehensive test of running ability on the athletic programme. The successful performer must have the speed of a quarter-miler and the endurance of a miler, combined in an event which is too long to run flat-out at any stage, yet too short to allow of any real slackening of the initial momentum. Moreover its brevity means that errors of pace judgement and tactics which might be capable of amendment in the course of a longer run, would here prove fatal to a runner's chances of winning.

The majority of great half-milers have been men of almost equivalent quarter-mile ability; a few milers of under-distance speed. Roger Moens is an outstanding example of versatility among half-milers with 47.3 secs for 400 metres, and 3 mins 58.9 secs for the mile. Herb Elliott, it will be noted, was Empire Games champion at both half-mile and mile. Both these runners however specialized in their favourite event in the Olympic Games. The build of the best half-milers is, like the sprinters, too varied to make any generalization, possible or relevant. Sydney Wooderson was 5 ft. 6 ins. in height and under 9 stone in weight. At the other extreme, Arthur Wint, Olympic 800 metres silver medallist in 1948 and 1952, was 6 ft. 4 in. and 13 stone. Peter Snell is 5 ft. 10 in. and 12½ stone.

Starting in the 880 yards has undergone a change in the last two years. Normally the runners line up according to the draw reading from the inside of the track on a line at right angles to the curb. This line is usually situated at the end of the straight. Sometimes the starting line forms an arc so that runners in outside berths are not at a dis-advantage. Since runners converging on the curb at the first turn have so often been in collision, a system of running the first turn in lanes was adopted and used at Rome. This meant staggered starts as in the 220 and 440 yards. Under the old system, a semi-crouch stance was usual, but at Rome most runners adopted a crouch start as in sprinting. It seems likely that the system of running the first turn in lanes will become more general so it is advisable for 880-yard men to practise crouch starts.

Tactics: in forming an idea of what constitutes good pace judgement, the runner cannot do better than consider intermediate times taken in certain record-breaking races.

Year	Name	Country	1st 440 secs	2nd 440 secs	880 min secs
1916	Ted Meredith	U.S.A.	52.8	59.4	1 52.2
1926	Otto Peltzer	Germany	54.6	57.0	1 51.6
1928	Sera Martin	France	52.8	57.8	1 50.6
1932	Tom Hampson	G.B.	55.0	54.8	1 49.8m
1938	Sydney Wooderson	G.B.	52.7	56.5	1 49.2
1939	Rudolph Harbig	Germany	53.0	53.6	1 46.6m
1948	Mal Whitfield	U.S.A.	54.0	55.2	1 49.2m
1950	Mal Whitfield	U.S.A.	50.5	58.7	1 49.2
1955	Roger Moens	Belgium	52.0	52.7	1 45.7m
1955	Audun Boysen	Norway	52.5e	53.4	1 45.9m
1957	Tom Courtney	U.S.A.	50.7	55.1	1 45.8m
1960	Peter Snell	N.Z.	52.5e	53.8	1 46.3m

m 800 metres race.

e estimated time.

The wide variations in pace shown in these figures makes it difficult to draw any general conclusions. It is worthy of note however that where the first lap has been run up to five seconds faster than the second, as in the case of Meredith (1916), Whitfield (1950), and Courtney (1957), it has been in a record attempt as such. In each case the runner was prepared to stake all and be more reckless with his resources than he would if competing against runners of equal calibre, who might have overtaken them in the second lap where deceleration was so marked. The times of Harbig, Moens, and Snell, were run more evenly, with the object of winning, and are therefore a better guide to good pace judgement in the half-mile.

A runner hoping to clock 2 mins for the half-mile could usefully treat 59 secs as an average pace for his first lap and as a unit for interval training. He might also attempt to run 660 yards in about 90 seconds in time trials. He will then have a basic knowledge of how to distribute his effort in a race but this will, of course, always be subject to the demands of positioning, a science learned only from competitive experience.

MONTH 1

Training programme for one week.

1st day. Free running 30–45 minutes, including stretches of striding up to about 600 yards.

2nd day. Track session. Warm up with 1 mile jogging, free exercises, 2–3 winders of 150 yards. Short rest. Interval running—6 × 220 or 4 × 440. Jogging to finish.

3rd day. Uphill running session. Warm up as before. 8–12 runs up 80 yards incline, jogging or walking down for recovery.

4th day. Free running.

5th day. Weight training or circuit training.

MONTH 2

Training programme for one week.

1st day. Free running 30 minutes.

2nd day. Track. Interval running—4 × 440 at better than 880 racing speed or 4 × 220 at close to top speed.

3rd day. Track. 2 × 660 yards time trials at 880 racing speed with 15 minutes rest.

4th day. Free running
5th day. Weight or circuit training.

The kind of training suitable for mid-season would follow the lines of the second and third days in Month 2. Competitive form will suggest whether to place the emphasis on speed work or stamina. An occasional race over 440 yards is a good way of easing the strain of weekly competition at 880 yards. Many runners find that competition once a fortnight is enough.

1 MILE   1500 METRES (1640.4 yards)

U.S. CHAMPION 1 MILE   Dyrol Burleson (at Eugene, Ore., 1961)   3 mins 57.6 secs
EMPIRE CHAMPION 1 MILE   Herb Elliott (Australia)
3 mins 59.0 secs
EUROPEAN CHAMPION 1500 METRES Brian Hewson (G.B.)
3 mins 41.9 secs
OLYMPIC CHAMPION 1500 METRES Herb Elliott (Australia)
3 mins 35.6 secs

(Approximate time differential between 1500 metres and 1 mile is 14-18 secs.)

Landmarks in mile history begin with the performances of Walter G. George, a Wiltshire man, who set an amateur record of 4 mins 18.4 secs in 1885, and a year later a professional record of 4 mins 12¾ secs. The latter mark was unbeaten by amateurs or professionals until Norman Taber gave America a marginal gain with 4 mins 12.6 secs in 1915. Real inroads were achieved in 1923 by the immortal 'Flying Finn', Paavo Nurmi, who clocked 4 mins 10.4 secs, and a year later 3 mins 52.6 secs for 1500 metres at which distance he also became Olympic champion at Paris.

The next human to hold both linear and metric records was the Frenchman, Jules Ladoumègue, who broke both the 4 mins 10 secs and 3 mins 50 secs barriers by exactly eight tenths of a second. The virtuosity of a New Zealander at Oxford, Jack Lovelock, accounted for further strides in both departments. Lovelock took the mile record to 4 mins 7.6 secs in 1934 and the 1500 metres to 3 mins 47.8 secs when dominating the Olympic final at Berlin in 1936. America's Glenn Cunningham, runner-up at Berlin, had sliced eight-tenths off his arch-rival's mile record in 1934, but lost this foothold to Sydney Wooderson who brought Great Britain the mile record again in 1937 with 4 mins 6.4 secs.

Neutral Sweden monopolized the creation of mile history during the war through the superb exploits of Gunder Hägg and Arne Andersson, who alternated in possession of the mile and 1500 metres records until disqualified for professional activities in 1945. Hägg had the last say with 4 mins 1.4 secs and 3 mins 43.0 secs among many other records. The latter mark was twice equalled, first by a former pacemaker of Hägg's, Lennart Strand, and later by Germany's Werner Lueg.

The first four-minute-mile, the most coveted performance in track history, was accomplished at 6 p.m. on the 6th May 1954. The runner was Roger Bannister of Great Britain, who ran four laps of the Iffley Road track at Oxford in 3 mins 59.4 secs to win the mile event in the O.U.A.C. versus A.A.A. match. Australia's John Landy soon eclipsed this record with a time of 3 mins 57.9 secs at Turku in Finland, but lost the Empire Games mile at Vancouver to Bannister in 3 mins 58.8 secs.

Landy's 1500 metres record of 3 mins 41.8 secs established *en route* in his great mile, underwent several renovations by European runners and appeared to have stabilized in 1957, when the Czech star, Stanislav Jungwirth, recorded 3 mins 38.1 secs. The same year Derek Ibbotson retrieved the mile record for Great Britain with 3 mins 57.2 secs, beating in the process both Jungwirth and the Melbourne Olympic 1500 metres champion, Ronnie Delany of Ireland.

But even these records were destined for only one year of life, for Herb Elliott effected the biggest single reduction since the inception of official records with a sensational 3 mins 54.5 secs at Dublin in 1958. A month later Elliott trimmed the 1500 metres best to 3 mins 36.0 secs at Göteborg, and in 1960 confirmed his massive supremacy by overwhelming the Olympic 1500 metres field in 3 mins 35.6 secs. The United Kingdom 1500 metres best of 3 mins 41.1 secs was set by Brian Hewson in a heat of the 1958 European Championship.

By the end of June 1961, 26 runners had broken four minutes for the mile 68 times, Elliott being the most prolific with 17 marks. Six Englishmen figure in this list— Ibbotson 3 mins 57.2 secs, Bannister 3 mins 58.8 secs, Hewson 3 mins 58.9 secs, Ken Wood 3 mins 59.3 secs, Chris Chataway 3 mins 59.8 secs, and Gordon Pirie 3 mins 59.9 secs.

It is impossible to generalize on the build of the best performers in the classic middle-distance event except perhaps to describe them all as being lean and wiry rather than muscularly powerful. Wooderson's small stature has been mentioned among half-milers. Bannister is 6 ft. 1½ in. and over 11 stone. Landy and Elliott a fraction under 6 ft. and nearer 10½ stone.

It is assumed that the general observations on middle distance at the beginning of Part Two have been absorbed together with the section on half-miling which contains much that is useful to the miler. However the mile has problems of its own and the greatest of these is pace judgement. Here again the intermediate times of record breakers will serve as a useful guide:

		Lap 1 secs	Lap 2 secs	Lap 3 secs	Lap 4 secs	Mile min/secs
1886	Walter George (G.B.)	58.5	63.5	65¾	65.0	4 12¾
1915	Norman Taber (U.S.A.)	58.0	67.0	68.0	59.6	4 12.6
1924	Paavo Nurmi (Finland)	58.6	63.2	64.9	63.7	4 10.4
1933	Jack Lovelock (N.Z.)	61.4	62.2	65.1	58.9	4 7.6
1937	Sydney Wooderson (G.B.)	58.6	64.0	64,6	59.2	4 6.4
1945	Gunder Hägg (Sweden)	56.5	62.7	62.2	60.0	4 1.4
1954	Roger Bannister (G.B.)	57.5	60.7	62.3	58.9	3 59.4
1954	John Landy (Australia)	58.5	60.2	58.5	60.7	*3 58.0
1957	Derek Ibbotson (G.B.)	56.0	60.4	63.9	56.9	3 57.2
1958	Herb Elliott (Australia)	56.4	61.8	61.0	55.3	3 54.5

* Clocked 3 mins 57.9 secs—returned as 3 mins 58.0 secs under the old rule requiring records over half-mile to be registered to the nearest fifth.

As in the half-mile it is evident here that perfect, even-pace running does not obtain in practice. The tendency of the early milers to use the second and third laps as a lull between a brisk opening and a hard-fought final lap has modified but not disappeared in modern miling. It is interesting to note that a similar distribution of effort was employed by both Wooderson and Bannister in specially paced record attempts where competition was not a relevant factor.

In most cases the record breaker preferred to follow for the greater part of his race. The exceptions were George, Hägg, and Landy. George set the pace until the third lap when his rival, Cummings, went into the lead only to collapse about 70 yards from home. Hägg raced straight into the lead in his memorable run at Malmö in 1945 and was never headed. Landy moved into the lead in the middle of the second lap in his world record. In the Empire Games mile at Vancouver in the same year, he led from the start but was overtaken by Bannister about 80 yards from the finish.

Lovelock, Bannister, and Ibbotson all made their finishing bursts between 200 and 300 yards from home, and in his world mile record in 1958, Elliott overtook his compatriot Merv Lincoln with about 500 yards to go. Elliott has shown a liking in many of his greatest races to dictate the pace from about the half-way mark. In the Olympic 1500 metres at Rome he was timed over the last 800 metres in 1 min 52.8 secs, in a sustained finishing drive to which, not surprisingly, his rivals had no answer.

In general the golden rule is to challenge for the lead as late as possible when the opposition have no time in which to respond. Occasional half-mile races are excellent tactical experience for the miler because all his problems can be met in the heightened tempo of a shorter distance, training him to think and react quicker to typical situations.

A runner hoping to clock 4 mins 30 secs for the mile could use 67 secs as his unit for 440-yard interval training, and 2 mins 15 secs as a basis for 880-yard intervals. In addition he might usefully put in speed work in 220-yard intervals at 30 secs, or well under his racing speed. Here again he will acquire pace judgement while getting fit, but will adapt his pace to the requirements of positioning in actual competition.

Month 1

Training programme for one week.

1st day. Free running 30–45 minutes, including stretches of striding up to 880 yards.

2nd day. Track session. Warm up with 1 mile jogging, free exercises, 2–3 winders 150 yards. Short rest. Interval running—6 × 440 or 3 × 880. Jogging to finish.

3rd day. Uphill running session. Warm up as before. 8–12 runs up 80-yard incline, jogging or walking down for recovery.

4th day. Free running.

5th day. Weight or circuit training.

Month 2

Training programme for one week.

1st day. Free running 30–45 minutes.

2nd day. Track session. Warm up. Interval running— 2 × 880 or 4 × 440. at better than mile racing speed, or 6 × 440 at mile racing speed. Jogging.

3rd day. Track. Warm up. 1 or 2 time trials over $\frac{3}{4}$ mile as for a race. Jogging.

4th day. Free running.
5th day. Weight or circuit training.

The kind of training suitable for mid-season would follow the lines of the second and third days in Month 2. Competition over the mile once a fortnight should be enough. Races over 880 yards are the best alternative, and occasionally a 2-mile race might be attempted. Conservation of energy is most important in distances over 880 yards and restraint will always pay dividends when choosing a programme of competition.

3000 METRES STEEPLECHASE
(1 mile 1520.88 yards)

(This event is not staged in the Empire Games)

U.S. CHAMPION	George Young (at Moscow, 1961)
	8 mins 38 secs
EUROPEAN CHAMPION	Jerzy Chromik (Poland)
	8 mins 38.2 secs
OLYMPIC CHAMPION	Zdzislaw Krzyskowiak (Poland)
	8 mins 34.2 secs

The earliest steeplechases were cross-country races of an unspecified but muddy nature which, even after they were introduced into track meetings late in the nineteenth century, were regarded as light entertainment rather than serious sport. Steeplechases of varied length were staged in the 1900, 1904, and 1908 Olympics but the 3000 metres distance was not recognized as the standard course until 1920. In that year Great Britain's Percy Hodge was the victor at Antwerp in the unhurried time of 10 mins 0.4 secs.

In 1924, Finland's Ville Ritola, who also won the 10,000

metres, started a long Finnish ascendancy by winning the
Olympic title in 9 mins 33.6 secs. Another illustrous Finn,
Volmari Iso-Hollo, won the Olympic steeplechase in 1932
over the odd distance of 3460 metres when Los Angeles
officials allowed the runners to complete an extra lap.
Iso-Hollo proved that this was no idle chance by regaining
his title at Berlin in 1936 in 9 mins 03.8 secs, this time over
the correct course.

The 9 min barrier was broken during the war by Sweden's
Erik Elmsäter but decisive inroads were not made on this
undeveloped event until 1952 when Russia's Vladimir
Kasantsev recorded a widely doubted 8 mins 46.8 secs.
That such things were quite possible was established one
month later when Kasantsev lost the Helsinki Olympic title
to Horace Ashenfelter of America in 8 mins 45.4 secs. In
third place was Britain's John Disley making his fourth
reduction of the best British performance with 8 mins
51.8 secs. Disley further improved to 8 mins 44.2 secs when
winning the steeplechase at the Great Britain versus Russia
match at Moscow in 1955. This equalled the listed world
record but Poland's Jerzy Chromik had a faster time
awaiting ratification and on the same day as Disley's run,
posted 8 mins 40.2 secs at Budapest.

The world record, only listed officially with effect from
1954 with Sandor Rosznyoi of Hungary the first tenant,
underwent several changes in 1955 and 1956 when Rosznyoi
again came into possession with 8 mins 35.6 secs. It therefore
came as a great and pleasing surprise when Britain's Chris
Brasher defeated him for the Melbourne Olympic title,
lowering the Olympic record and the British best to 8 mins
41.2 secs in the process.

Chromik came into his own again in 1958 setting his
third world record in 8 mins 32.0 secs and winning the

European title at Stockholm. He was however eclipsed in 1960 by his compatriot Krzyskowiak who reached a new level of 8 mins 31.3 secs and attached his name to the roll of Olympic gold medallists at Rome. Russia's Grigori Taran cut another tenth from the world record in 1961.

The physical qualities of the steeplechaser are no different from those of the good miler and three-miler. The race is, of course, a middle-distance event with obstacles thrown in. Technique is secondary and economy of action, endurance, pace judgement, and tactics the important factors in success. It is worth noting that the best steeplechasers have not been pure specialists. Chris Brasher played a well-known role in the first four-minute mile, and on the eve of his Melbourne triumph, won a two-mile race in strong International company. The Olympic champion, Krzyskowiak, was European Champion at 5000 and 10,000 metres. It follows that no steeplechaser of the future will be great without reaching the top flight at two and three miles.

This requirement fits in with the tendency of steeplechasers to compete very rarely in their speciality. The jarring nature of the course makes it inadvisable to undergo the full ordeal more often than perhaps six times in a season. Steeplechasers sometimes race over half the distance, that is in 1500 metres steeplechases, or more often they keep in touch with the best middle-distance men over one or two miles, and perhaps even longer distances.

Measurements: in the 3000 metres steeplechase there are twenty-eight 3-ft. hurdles and seven water jumps. The hurdles are of heavy timber which cannot be overturned, and the water jump consists of a 3-ft. solid hurdle followed by the water jump, 12 ft. square, with water to a depth of 2 ft. 6 in. at the hurdle end diminishing to the level of the track at the exit end. The following is a specification for distribution of the obstacles:

	Yds.	Yds.
Distance from start to beginning of lap one, to be run without jumps		270
Distance from beginning of lap one to first hurdle	10	
From first to second hurdle	86	
From second to third hurdle	86	
From third hurdle to water jump	86	
From water jump to fourth hurdle	86	
From fourth hurdle to finishing line	76	
	430	
Seven laps at 430 yards		3010
	Total	3280

(equivalent to 3000 metres)

The length of each full lap is 430 yards because the approach and run-off from the water jump is normally situated inside the turn on a standard 440 yards circuit.

Technique: hurdle clearance as described in Part Two need not be dwelt on again here except to state that it is of very great importance in an event with twenty-eight hurdles. Ideally the hurdles should be taken in a style consistent with the pace and rhythm of the race as a whole, that is without the exaggerated dip and snap down of sprint hurdling which would clearly be uneconomical in a middle distance. As the hurdles are placed 86 yards apart stride precision is not possible so the athlete should practise running at a 3-ft.

hurdle from varying distances in order to acquire a good eye for stride adjustment, and of course, if he can learn to hurdle off either foot, he will be more flexible in competitive conditions. The hurly-burly of running in a pack makes efficient hurdling a tricky task, and it is essential to hold a good position on the approach to a hurdle where collisions can be fatal to balance. It is also essential to try and clear the obstacle wide of any challenging opponent to avoid the hindrance of an arm swing over the hurdle, upsetting the 'chaser's balance on landing.

Considerations of positioning apply equally to the approach to the water jump, but here technique must be more precise and deliberate because of the far more severe nature of the obstacle. Practice should first be carried out in the absence of a water jump, a twelve-foot line on the track being sufficient to indicate the point on the track corresponding to the far edge of the water. Since clearance of hurdle and water constitute a powerful effort they must be approached at a good speed and with unfaltering stride for at least the last 15 yards. After several tentative runs a check mark can be established at that distance which can always serve in competition as the range from which take-off can be reached in a known number of regular strides.

It will be found that the approximate distance of the take-off from the hurdle is five feet. Having rehearsed the approach to a fair degree of consistency, clearance can now be tackled. The technique is a two-stage jump, the first being a step up on to the top surface of the hurdle which is five inches wide, the second a leap into the shallow end of the water, landing on the take-off foot. As confidence is gained in the step-up stage, the step-down can be developed. The leg taking the weight on the hurdle bar should be flexed to provide leverage for thrust as the body weight passes the upright. At the same time the co-ordinating arm should be checked and brought through strongly to assist the forward drive of the landing leg and the overall impetus out of the water.

Having practised hurdling and water jumping regularly in preliminary training, the steeplechaser will find that there are many points which can be perfected. Hurdle training at faster than racing pace will quicken the eye for stride adjustment and make it easier to adjust in the slower rhythm of a full 3000 metres. It is a good thing to cultivate a slight acceleration in the last few strides to a hurdle, as well as to the water jump, to ensure a good clearance particularly when fatigue may have temporarily impaired judgement of distances a little. The hurdle clearance should have the feel of a movement which has departed from normal running style only enough to allow the hurdle to pass under the runner's centre of gravity.

A refinement which many good steeplechasers adopt is the use of a handful of white powder or chalk to make a distinctive mark on the approach to the water jump indicating their familiar check point. Constant step-up practice can enable the athlete to place his foot on the bar in such a way that his spikes overlap the far edge and provide additional purchase for his clearance thrust. Landing and exit from the water must be studied closely. Most water jumps have coconut- or rubber-matting under water in the landing area which makes landing secure and getaway speedy. The landing leg should be slightly flexed to give impetus to the exit stride and obviate stumbling on the incline. The trailing leg must assist this process by being lifted high into the next stride. A good steeplechaser will only get one foot wet in the course of seven water-jump clearances.

Training for condition: as mentioned at the beginning of Part Three, all middle-distance events have the same basic training principles so the steeplechaser will get fit on the same lines as the one- and three-miler with, of course, regular work on hurdling and water jumping included in his programme. It is therefore not necessary to repeat the suggested two-month training programme in full for the steeplechaser can readily draw up a suitable schedule based on one- and three-mile schedules, particularly as he will be training with runners specializing in those events.

3 MILES   5000 METRES (3 mile 188.2 yards)

U.S. CHAMPION 3 MILES   Max Truex (at London, 1961)
13 mins 21.0 secs
EMPIRE CHAMPION 3 MILES   Murray Halberg (N.Z.)
13 mins 15.0 secs
EUROPEAN CHAMPION 5000 METRES   Z. Krzyszkowiak
(Poland)   13 mins 53.4 secs
OLYMPIC CHAMPION 5000 METRES Murray Halberg (N.Z.)
13 mins 43.4 secs

(Approximate time differential between 3 miles and 5000 metres is 25-30 secs.)

In 1903, Alfred Shrubb, one of Britain's most versatile distance champions, set a world 3-mile record of 14 mins 17.6 secs. It took Paavo Nurmi 20 years later to remove this mark with 14 mins 11.2 secs at Stockholm. Nurmi also added to his catalogue of records with a 5000 metres world best of 14 mins 28.2 secs and became Olympic titlist at that distance in 1924 at Paris. Another Finn, Hannes Kolehmainen, had won the 5000 metres when it first appeared in the Olympic programme in 1912. A third Finn, Lauri Lehtinen, succeeded Nurmi in the record books and on the

Olympic roll of honour in 1932. Lehtinen started a fashion of breaking records in pairs when setting a 3-mile record of 13 mins 50.6 secs and running on to reach the 5000 metres post in 14 mins 17.0 secs. The last Finn to lead the world was Taisto Mäki, who in 1939 produced marks of 13 mins 42.4 secs and 14 mins 8.8 secs in the course of the same race.

The war gave neutral Sweden scope for progress and it was again the tireless legs of Gundar Hägg which demonstrated the inadequacy of previous records. Hägg spared time from miling to run 5000 metres in 13 mins 59.8 secs having passed the 3 miles in 13 mins 32.4 secs at Gothenburg in 1942.

At home, Shrubb's record for 3 miles was finally reduced in 1936 by Peter Ward. Ward set a native record of 14 mins 15.8 secs but like many Englishmen excelled himself abroad to run 14 mins 2.0 secs for 3 miles and 14 mins 31.6 secs for 5000 metres at Helsinki in 1937. Sydney Wooderson came back to longer distances after the war with sterling results. He ran 13 mins 53.2 secs when winning the A.A.A. 3 miles title in 1946, and a month later became European 5000 metres champion in 14 mins 8.6 secs.

Emil Zatopek, the Czech phenomenon, now assumed the mastery of the world scene, narrowly losing the 1948 Olympic 5000 metres and winning it decisively in 1952. He failed however to match Hägg's world mark which survived until 1954 when Russia's Vladimir Kuts toppled Zatopek and the record in winning the European title with 13 mins 56.6 secs. The Hägg 3-mile record went the same year when Freddie Green won the A.A.A. 3 miles from Chris Chataway in the shared world record time of 13 mins 32.2 secs. Chataway became Empire Games champion only to be beaten by Kuts for the European title, but turned the tables on him in a spectacular floodlit duel at White City, shearing five seconds from the world 5000 metres record. The durable Russian however made his reply within days with a 13 mins 51.2 secs performance at Prague.

Chataway came further into his own in 1955 with a world 3 miles record of 13 mins 23.2 secs. This he surrendered to Hungary's Sandor Iharos who also dispossessed Kuts with a metric 13 mins 40.6 secs. A period of months sufficed to bring about a fresh level this time through the efforts of Gordon Pirie. Pirie had succeeded Wooderson in the British 3-mile record lists but was temporarily overshadowed by Chataway. In 1956 he rose to unprecedented heights of fame at Bergen in Norway by inflicting a memorable defeat on Kuts in a world record 13 mins 36.8 secs. Kuts ran 13 mins 39.6 secs in second place, a time which later that year enabled him to beat Pirie for the Olympic title at Melbourne. Kuts had a final say over 5000 metres in 1957 with a virtually solo 13 mins 35.0 secs at Rome, while the world 3 miles record was lowered to a comparable 13 mins 10.8 secs by Australia's Albie Thomas in 1958.

The United Kingdom 3 miles best passed from Chataway to Derek Ibbotson who, failing to qualify for the 1957 A.A.A. 1 mile final, ran instead in the 3 miles to register 13 mins 20.8 secs. In 1960 Bruce Tulloh, running barefooted and on grass, was timed at an astonishing 13 mins 17.2 secs. Pirie clocked 13 mins 16.4 secs in 1961.

6 MILES   10,000 METRES (6 miles 376.39 yards)

U.S. CHAMPION 6 MILES   Al Lawrence (at Houston, Tex., 1960)   28 mins 35.8 secs
EMPIRE CHAMPION 6 MILES   Dave Power (Australia) 28 mins 47.8 secs

EUROPEAN CHAMPION 10,000 METRES
Zdzislaw Krzyskowiak (Poland)
28 mins 56.0 secs
OLYMPIC CHAMPION 10,000 METRES   Pyotr Bolotnikov
(Russia)   28 mins 32.2 secs

(Approximate time differential between 6 miles and 10,000 metres is 55–65 secs.)

Alfred Shrubb was responsible for one of the earliest 6-mile records in 1904 with a 29 mins 59.4 secs. The first official world record for 10,000 metres was held by France's Jean Bouin whose name is commemorated at a stadium in Paris, with 30 mins 58.8 secs in 1911. Finland's Hannes Koleh-mainen won the Olympic title at Stockholm in 1912 but his time fell short of Bouin's doubtless because he was busy winning other titles. Paavo Nurmi next assumed the mantle of Finnish supremacy, taking the 1920 and 1928 Olympic titles but leaving his compatriot Ville Ritola to win the 1924 gold medal in 30 mins 23.2 secs, a time which improved Ritola's own world record. One month after the Games Nurmi, who had been well-occupied at Paris winning four other titles, re-claimed the 10,000 metres record in decisive style with 30 mins 6.2 secs. As an after-thought he clipped Shrubb's 6-mile record, which had for 20 years received little attention, to 29 mins 36.4 secs shortly before his suspension for professionalism in 1930.

Though Finns occupied second and third places it was a Pole, Janus Kusocinski, who in 1932 captured the Los Angeles Olympic 10,000 metres title. Nurmi's world record however survived until a new Finn, Ilmari Salminen, improved to 30 mins 5.6 secs in 1937, a year after he had become Olympic champion. Taisto Mäki proved himself as great in the longer distances as he had at 5000 metres and would have been a certain Olympic winner had war not intervened at the height of his career.

The British records of Alfred Shrubb were on the lists until 1936 when J. A. Burns made new marks at metres and yards which held until Dr Frank Aaron's 1950 records of 29 mins 43.2 secs for 6 miles and 30 mins 31.6 secs for 10,000 metres. The last of the great Finns, Viljo Heino had meanwhile been busy making vast inroads into the world records not only at these distances but at 10 miles and beyond. Following the wartime dearth of athletic history Heino's feats were regarded as almost unbelievable but the appearance of the Czech marvel Emil Zatopek opened fresh horizons. Zatopek ran away with the Olympic 10,000 metres titles at Wembley and Helsinki, and reduced the world record in five instalments to 28 mins 54.2 secs. Two European titles at this distance and a host of longer records gave the Czech a catalogue of fame equalled only by Nurmi's.

The world 6-mile record was held briefly by Britain's Gordon Pirie who posted the first of his five world marks in winning the 1953 A.A.A. title in 28 mins 19.4 secs. This was improved by Zatopek but figured in the British lists for three years until taken over by Ken Norris, the first Englishman to have won the New Year's Eve road race at São Paolo, Brazil. Police Constable Stan Eldon was responsible in 1958 for British best times of 28 mins 5.0 secs for 6 miles and 29 mins 2.8 secs for 10,000 metres, the latter record passing to the Welshman John Merriman when finishing eighth in the Rome final in 28 mins 52.6 secs. Martin Hyman took the U.K. 6 miles record to 27 mins 54.4 secs in 1961.

Proving that the longer the distance, the more slack there

is to take in, Sandor Iharos sliced 12 secs from Zatopek's world 10,000 metres record in 1956, only to suffer within months a similar demotion by Russia's Vladimir Kuts who ran a startling 28 mins 30.4 secs before going to Melbourne to win the Olympic title. Iharos remained the holder of the less popular 6-mile record in 27 mins 43.8 secs, but it took another Russian, Pyotr Bolotnikov, to succeed Kuts as world 10,000 metres record holder with 28 mins 18.8 secs.

The 3 and 6 miles present no problems not found in the mile except the obvious one of greater mileage. The tactical aspects of middle-distance are less urgent, and economy and endurance the preponderant factors in success. For convenience I have linked the 3 miles with the 6 miles, and many runners combine the two. Many great 3-milers, including Halberg, Thomas, Pirie, Ibbotson, and Chataway have broken four minutes for the mile. Others, like Zatopek and Kuts, have been moderate milers but stronger in the 6-mile range and therefore able to take the 3 miles in their stride. A very few, like Halberg, Pirie, and Iharos, have reached world class at all three distances. On the biggest occasions however it has been the two longer distances in which the doubles have been achieved. Zatopek and Kuts had Olympic doubles at 5000 and 10,000 metres, and Halberg took the 3 and 6 miles in the Empire Games. In view of Bolotnikov's resounding success in the Olympic 10,000 metres it is likely, too, that he could have been in the medals at 5000 metres had he taken part.

Bearing in mind the need for economy, the significant physical fact about all these great double winners is that they are men of small stature. Bolotnikov is 5 ft. 8 in. and a shade under 10 stone. Halberg is 5 ft. 11 in. and $9\frac{1}{2}$ stone. Zatopek was perhaps even smaller while Kuts, though heavier than the others, was only 5 ft. 7½ in. tall. It is almost certain, incidentally, that none of them could have been successful at any other athletic event owing to their physical limitations. The small man who does not have much natural speed, but is prepared to do the hard work, will often find his metier in the long distances. Significantly, most great distance runners are at their best nearer the age of thirty than twenty-five, proving that results in this most exacting department of athletics are achieved only by prolonged application.

Tactics: the fundamental laws of even pace and positioning are perhaps even more relevant to the long distances, where losing contact with the leaders or rash pace distribution have greater scope in ruining a man's chances of winning. Contact with the opposition in fact is the all-important aspect of long distance tactics because the sheer ordeal of protracted effort is made far more severe by isolation. This apparently innocuous truth is based on very sound physical and psychological reasons. It has been proved that the pain messages conveyed to the brain in times of fatigue are received far in advance of the limit of a man's capabilities. This means that although he may be suffering excruciatingly and feel himself to be on the point of collapse, his body is a long way from being really tired. Obviously the close proximity of a rival helps a runner to feel that he can keep going, particularly if he is following the pace and getting the benefit of a rival's slipstream. This is why a front runner will often throw considerations of even pace to the winds and put in apparently suicidal bursts of speed in the middle of a long race, to drop a close-following opponent and deprive him of the psychological advantage of his presence.

Perhaps the best-known example of this was the Chataway-Kuts duel at White City in 1954. Kuts knew that he would have to sap Chataway's superior finishing power by breakaway tactics during the race if he were to win. He, in fact, gained leads of up to eight yards in this way, but each time Chataway, who had resolutely dogged his footsteps from the gun, slowly regained his position in the Russian's shadow. Then in the closing strides he came by with a superbly timed finishing dash.

Kuts applied the same tactics in his Olympic double at Melbourne, though there no one could withstand his break-away bursts. He finished both races in an isolation made more secure by the certainty that he had snapped the psychological link which at White City had made it possible for Chataway to master him.

Both Halberg and Bolotnikov used similar tactics at Rome, breaking away in the last 1000 metres of their respective races and holding on to the gap from their detached rivals.

The following are intermediate times taken in record-breaking distance races:

Olympic 5000 metres, Melbourne 1956, won by Vladimir Kuts who led almost throughout.

fastest lap—the 1st	62.2 secs
slowest lap—the 5th	67.0 ,,
last lap	62.7 ,,

1st 1000 metres	2 mins	40.1 secs
2nd 1000 ,,	2 ,,	46.1 ,,
3rd 1000 ,,	2 ,,	45.0 ,,
4th 1000 ,,	2 ,,	46.2 ,,
5th 1000 ,,	2 ,,	42.1 ,,
Total time	13 ,,	39.5 ,,

Olympic record.

Chataway-Kuts duel, White City, 1954 (Kuts's times quoted since he led most of the way)

1st lap—	62.8 secs
last lap fastest—Kuts	60.4 secs
Chataway	60.1 secs

1st 1000 metres	2 mins 41.4 secs
2nd 1000 ,,	2 ,, 50.1 ,,
3rd 1000 ,,	2 ,, 44.9 ,,
4th 1000 ,,	2 ,, 53.4 ,,
5th 1000 ,,	2 ,, 42.0 ,,
Kuts's final time	13 ,, 51.8 ,,
Chataway's final time	13 ,, 51.6 ,,
	world record.

Olympic 10,000 metres, Melbourne, 1956: won by Kuts, who led throughout.

fastest lap—1st	61.5 secs
slowest lap—16th	73.2 ,,
last lap	66.6 ,,

1st 2000 metres	5 mins 31.8 secs
2nd 2000 ,,	5 ,, 44.7 ,,
3rd 2000 ,,	5 ,, 45.8 ,,
4th 2000 ,,	5 ,, 58.7 ,,
5th 2000 ,,	5 ,, 44.6 ,,
final time	28 ,, 45.6 ,,
	Olympic record.

Kuts's intermediate 5000 metres time was 14 mins 6.8 secs, only 0.2 secs outside Zatopek's 1952 Olympic 5000 metres record.

Olympic 5000 metres, Rome 1960: won by Murray Halberg.

fastest lap the 9th	61.8 secs		
slowest lap the last	73.0 secs		

1st 1000 metres Zimny leading	2 mins 41.2 secs
2nd 1000	,,	Thomas	,,	2 ,, 47.0 ,,
3rd 1000	,,	Zimny	,,	2 ,, 51.2 ,,
4th 1000	,,	Halberg	,,	2 ,, 52.3
5th 1000	,,			2 ,, 41.7
final time				13 ,, 43.4 ,,

Murray Halberg's record attempt at 3 miles and 5000 metres at Stockholm, 25th July 1961.

1st 400 metres	64.0 secs			
1st 1000	,,	2 mins 41.4 ,,		
2nd 1000	,,	2 ,, 46.6 ,,		
3rd 1000	,,	2 ,, 43.4 ,,		
4th 1000	,,	2 ,, 46.6 ,,		
5th 1000	,,	2 ,, 37.2 ,,		
3 mile time	13 ,, 10.0 ,,	(world record)		
5000 metres time	13 ,, 35.2 ,,	(0.2 secs outside world record)		

Training: the longer the competitive distance the further a man must cover in training, so the 3- and 6-miler will need to work on a schedule similar to that suggested for the miler with the distances extended. Interval running in units of quarter, half, and one mile should form the basis of track training, but by far the greater proportion of the distance man's work should be free running. In order to reduce the monotony, cross-country running is probably the best way of getting in the kind of mileage needed.

Bolotnikov was reported to have run over 2,500 miles in training during 1960. This meant a weekly average of about 50 miles throughout the year, and of course this mileage will have been exceeded quite easily at the height of training. Though this may seem to be the last word in drudgery, masses of pure running is the only way to acquire the mental and physical endurance for the long distances. A man like Bolotnikov who daily comes face-to-face with this kind of hard work in the course of prolonged training stints, develops a familiarity with the symptoms of fatigue amounting almost to contempt. Only by constant and relentless application can a runner penetrate deeper into the no-man's land between his apparent and his real physical limit. There is absolutely and literally no short cut.

Competition: the heavy drain of long-distance racing makes frequent competition out of the question, though an occasional spate of racing is essential in preparation for the big events where there may be preliminaries to contest. Generally, distance runners rest from competing over their speciality by entering in shorter races of 1 or 2 miles where they feel they have nothing to lose if they get beaten and something to gain in terms of speed training. Many distance runners compete in cross-country events though most of them admit that they treat it as a variant in training rather than as a specialized event. There is no doubt too that the more informal and friendly nature of cross-country and also of road-racing events, make them an attractive workout for the distance man. It is very rarely that a runner has a really successful track season following a good cross-country and road-racing winter. Many good runners, one suspects, have in fact lost their form through trying to climb too many Everests and competing as though their life depended on it all the year round.

Restraint is therefore the best policy in choosing a long-distance runner's programme of competition, but since experience must be gained the hard way, a fortnightly race over the speciality, alternating with a fortnightly race of shorter distance may be a reasonable balance. In any case, the old adage that a man must have travelled before he can arrive, is emphatically relevant to success in this toughest of all individual sports.

Left: U.S.A. v. U.S.S.R. match, Moscow, 1961: Vitold Kreyer, Olympic bronze medallist at Rome, wins the triple jump with 54 ft. 8¼ ins.
Right: Milan, 1961: Carlo Lievore (Italy) sets a world javelin record of 284 ft. 7 ins.

Left: Olympic hammer competition, Rome, 1960: the left-handed Vasiliy Rudenkov (U.S.S.R.), who won the title. *Right:* Great Britain v. Hungary match, White City, 1960: Gyula Zsivotzky (Hungary), the Rome Olympic silver medallist, completing his final turn.

Left: Ol.mpic shot put competition, Rome, 1960: Bill Nieder (U.S.A.), the champion, packs a punch behind the 16 lb. ball.
Right: Arthur **Rowe**, Empire and European champion, who reached third place in the all-time list in 1961 with a put of 64 ft. 2 ins. at Mansfield.

Above: Olympic discus competition, Rome, 1960: Al Oerter (U.S.A.) makes full use of the concrete circle. Oerter retained the title which he had won at Melbourne in 1956.

Right: Great Britain v. Hungary match, White City, 1961: Jozsef Szecsenyi (Hungary) unleashes a winning discus. Distance 187 ft. 3½ ins.

Left: Zdzislaw Krzyskowiak (Poland), who set a world 3,000 metres steeplechase record of 8 mins. 30·4 secs. in 1961. *Right:* Olympic 5,000 metres final, Rome, 1960: Murray Halberg (N.Z.) wins in 13 mins. 43·4 secs., with Hans Grodotzki (Germany) second, and Kazimierz Zimny (Poland) third.

Above: Olympic 10,000 metres final, Rome, 1960: Pyotr Bolotnikov (U.S.S.R.) lies second, with Hans Grodotzki (Germany), No. 277, who finished second, down the field at this stage. Bolotnikov's winning time, 28 mins. 32·2 secs., Olympic record. *Below:* Great Britain v. U.S.A. match, 3 miles, White City, 1961: Max Truex (U.S.A.) leads from Gordon Pirie and Bruce Tulloh. Pirie's winning time, 13 mins. 16·4 secs., United Kingdom National record.

Olympic 1,500 metres final, Rome, 1960: Herb Elliott leads from Istvan Rozsavölgyi (Hungary), Michel Jazy (France), and Zoltan Vamos (Rumania). Elliott's winning time, 3 mins. 35·6 secs., Olympic and world record.

Above: England v. Russian F.R., White City, 1961; 3,000 metres steeplechase: Nikolay Sokolov, the winner, takes the water jump, with Maurice Herriott (2) lying third. Sokolov set a United Kingdom all-comers record of 8 mins. 40·6 secs.; and Herriott an A.A.A. National record of 8 mins. 42·0 secs. *Below:* European Championships, Stockholm, 1958: Jerzy Chromik (Poland), No. 239, takes a hurdle in the heats of the 3,000 metres steeplechase.

PART FOUR

Jumping and Vaulting

HIGH JUMP

U.S. CHAMPION	John Thomas (at Palo Alto, Cal., 1960) 7 ft. 3¾ in.
EMPIRE CHAMPION	Ernie Haisley (Jamaica) 6 ft. 9 in.
EUROPEAN CHAMPION	Rickard Dahl (Sweden) 6 ft. 11½ in.
OLYMPIC CHAMPION	Robert Shavlakadze (U.S.S.R.) 7 ft. 1 in.

When in 1876 M. J. Brooks became the first human officially to clear 6 ft. in bona fide competition, some thought the feat impossible. None the less Brooks got over 6 ft. 2½ in. only eighteen days later, and in the following month took the English championship unopposed at 6 ft. The greatest nineteenth-century jumper was an Irish-American named M. F. Sweeney who in 1895 cleared 6 ft. 5⅝ in. using a modified scissors, a feat which would baffle most modern exponents. The early Olympians were far inferior to Sweeney; the winners in the first four celebrations, all Americans, mustering nothing better than 6 ft. 3 in. In 1912 America's George Horine invented the 'Western roll' which enabled him to set a world record of 6 ft. 7 in. He was however beaten into third place at the Stockholm Games that year by his compatriot Alva Richards with 6 ft. 4 in.

At home Brooks's record was forty-four years old when B. Howard Baker, the soccer international, first improved on it with 6 ft. 3¼ in. Baker's best of 6 ft. 5 in. in 1921 was to defy renovation for a further twenty-eight years.

The most celebrated jumper of the twenties was Harold

Osborn, who elevated the world record to 6 ft. 8¼ in., and in the same year, 1924, collected the Olympic high jump and decathlon titles for America. Osborn's Olympic record survived two Olympiads and his world mark for an even longer span until raised in two increments to 6 ft. 9⅛ in. by Walter Marty. A gangling American negro, Cornelius Johnson, was the Olympic titlist in 1936 defeating another American negro, Dave Albritton, who earlier that year had shared 'Corny's' new world record of 6 ft. 9¾ in. Thirteen months sufficed to bring about the arrival of a new American negro, Mel Walker, at the summit with 6 ft. 10⅜ in.

A height of 6 ft. 11 in., cleared in 1941, coming as it did during the war, probably did not represent the ultimate of Lester Steers, but this remained inviolate until Walter Davis, like Steers a white American, added half an inch in 1953. The possibility of jumping 7 ft. was now beyond doubt since both Steers and Davis had been over in training. The first official clearance however came from Charlie Dumas who went over 7 ft. 0½ in. in 1956, and like Davis, followed with an Olympic title.

American supremacy in the world lists underwent its first setback since official history began in 1912, when Russia's Yuriy Stepanov straddled over 7 ft. 1⅛ in. in 1957. The ban on built-up shoes in 1958 cramped Russian progress for two years which was time enough for a new American prodigy, John Thomas, to burst on the scene with an astonishing over 7 ft. series culminating in a 7 ft. 3¾ in. ascent at Palo Alto in July 1960. For all this, Thomas was obliged to accept a bronze medal at Rome when Russia effected the third breach in American domination in Olympic history (Canada's Duncan McNaughton in 1932, and Australia's John Winter in 1948). Then to the amazement of the athletic world, Valeriy Brumel, who had shared his countryman's winning height in Rome to win a silver medal, lifted Thomas's world record to a dizzy 7 ft. 4½ in. indoors at Leningrad in January 1961.

The United Kingdom record passed from Baker to a lofty Scot named Alan Paterson who reached 6 ft. 7½ in. in 1947, a mark equalled by Peter Wells in 1954. Another Scot, Crawford Fairbrother, took over the business of record breaking in 1959, his most recent instalment having been indoors at Stanmore where he cleared 6 ft. 9 in. in 1961.

The high jump demands physique allied to technique to an extent that perhaps more than in any other event, one cannot lead to success without the other. Jumping ability is definitely related to physical stature. John Thomas at 6 ft. 5½ in. is an outstanding example of natural talent while Valeriy Brumel who is probably the best exponent technically, is 6 ft. 0½ in. tall. The following table shows that

Name and country	Height jumped ft. in.	Personal height ft. in.	Difference in.
Valeriy Brumel (U.S.S.R.)	7 4½	6 0½	16
John Thomas (U.S.A.)	7 3¾	6 5¾	10
Robert Shavlakadze (U.S.S.R.)	7 1	6 1¼	11¾
Viktor Bolshov (U.S.S.R.)	7 0¾	6 0	12¾
Charles Dumas (U.S.A.)	7 0⅝	6 1	11⅜
Joe Faust (U.S.A.)	7 0	5 11⅝	12⅜

the best performers can jump more than a foot over their own height so it can be stated almost categorically that further advances will come from taller men.

Development of Technique: the object of technique in the high jump is to exploit natural spring to the maximum by keeping the body's centre of gravity as low as possible in clearance. The simple scissor jump of Brooks and the

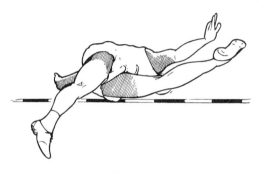

Figure 10

early jumpers meant crossing the bar in an upright sitting position. Sweeney employed a twist which brought his upper body down and his hips up on crossing the bar. This originated on the east coast of America and became known as the 'Eastern Cut-Off' (Fig. 10). Horine found that by taking off from the foot nearest the bar he could roll over on his side and effect a more efficient clearance. Since he evolved this at Stanford University on the west coast of America, this was called the 'Western Roll' (Fig. 11).

Perhaps the earliest jumper to have used something approximating to the modern 'straddle' was the renowned and versatile star of women's sport 'Babe' Didrikson. She cleared 5 ft. $5\frac{1}{4}$ in. at the Los Angeles Olympics with what she called the 'California Roll', but this was not allowed as a world record because it was a head-first dive. Later this rule was amended and a jump was deemed fair providing it was accomplished off one foot. The great majority of good jumpers today, certainly all those who have cleared 7 ft., are straddle jumpers.

The Rules: the uprights must be rigid and between 12 ft. and 13 ft. $2\frac{1}{4}$ in. apart. The bar must be metal or wood of uniform thickness and section to a diameter of not more than $1\frac{1}{4}$ in., between 11 ft. $11\frac{1}{4}$ in. and 13 ft. $1\frac{1}{2}$ in. long and no heavier than 4 lb. $6\frac{2}{3}$ oz. with black and white zebra stripes for better sighting. Flat rectangular pegs, $1\frac{1}{2}$ in. by $2\frac{3}{8}$ in., support the bar in such a way that it is in contact with each peg for not more than two inches and is capable of being pushed off on either the approach or pit side of the uprights. The take-off fan should be at least 50 ft. in diameter and the pit 16 ft. by 12 ft. filled preferably with

Figure 11

wood shavings or sorbo rubber chunks, and ideally built up to make the impact of landing less heavy.

In competition the jumpers take part in the order listed on the programme starting at a pre-arranged height, and ascending in increments determined at the end of each round. A jumper is allowed three attempts at each height, but may reserve himself for a subsequent height after less than three attempts if he wishes, always subject to the proviso that three consecutive failures at whatever height eliminates him from the competition. This applies even if only one competitor remains in the competition, his last

Figure 12

valid clearance being the winning performance. Measurements to the nearest $\frac{1}{4}$ in. must be made with a steel tape between the ground and the lowest point of the bar.

In the event of a tie, the jumper with the fewest attempts at the winning height is first. If a tie still exists the competitor with fewest failures throughout the contest wins. If there is still a tie, the jumper with the fewest attempts, successful or otherwise, up to the last height cleared, gains the verdict. Any further ties are resolved by competition at decreasing heights until a decision is reached.

Training for technique: the straddle, when correctly performed, is the best method because it allows the jumper's centre of gravity to pass under the bar. The scissor jump (Fig. 12) is the most wasteful method with the centre of gravity travelling nearly a foot over the bar. The straddle by contrast achieves a drape-over layout which does actually make the most of natural spring.

The run-up should be long enough to generate the maximum impetus that can be controlled and converted into upward leverage. This in practice is from five to nine strides which should be smoothly graduated to produce the greatest accuracy on the desired point of take-off. The length of approach is a matter for individual experiment and will require adjustment in the light of prevailing track and weather conditions. The angle of approach must be established by repeated experiment. Figure 13 shows an approximate take-off pattern for a left-footed jumper. Precise approach routine is essential because the path of the jumper's clearance is decided at take-off and cannot be

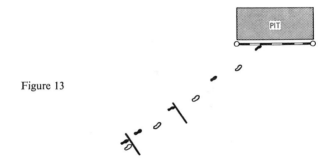

Figure 13

changed in the air where only minor movements are carried out. The main problem at take-off is to resolve upward spring and body rotation in the best way. Some vertical impetus must be wasted in the process of launching the body into the straddle, but correctly performed, it should result in a net gain.

The last stride of the approach should be relaxed and constitute a gather as the jumper rolls from heel to toe. The free leg, in this case the right, swings vigorously towards the far upright assisted by a concerted simultaneous lift from both arms. The right arm and foot cross the bar first, and the head, the heaviest mass in the body, is pushed over. The weight of head and shoulders descending will create a reaction at the point of fullest drape by hoisting the hips and trailing leg to their greatest elevation. The trailing leg must be whipped clear of the bar as the jumper drops, by turning it outwards to complete the rotational movement that has taken the jumper over the bar while his centre of gravity passes under. The jumper will land on his side, or possibly on his back, emphasizing the importance of having a soft, built-up pit.

Training for condition: obviously the performance of a good straddle requires bodily suppleness and powerful spring which in turn demands muscular strength. The protracted nature of many competitions demands a third quality of the jumper, stamina. Exercises for suppleness, similar to those recommended for hurdling on page 43, should form part of the jumper's warming-up period before every training session. Winders and sprints should also be carried out as described in the section on sprinting. The hardest track work should be reserved for the end of a training session, for technique is easier to assimilate when the muscles are still fresh. Weight and circuit training will not, as some believe, impair natural spring. On the contrary under experienced supervision, these activities increase strength and contribute directly to jumping power. John Thomas and Valeriy Brumel are both regular weight trainers, in and out of season.

As in other technique events, there is a limit to the

amount of jumping that a learner can usefully do in one outing. His jumps should be in groups of perhaps three or four with a break for rest or change of activity preceding the next set of jumps. The track work, which is recommended for the end of a session, might include sprinting and low hurdling, or any other event in which the jumper has a secondary interest. Many jumpers play basket ball. All these can contribute to his overall fitness and stamina, but the best results will ultimately be achieved by specialization.

It is doubtful whether real technical skill can be acquired without a coach but the individual can keep an eye on his own progress by attention to certain details. In perfecting the run up, two check marks are useful, one at the start, and another after three strides. This helps the business of reaching take-off with pin-point accuracy. When warming-up, a few easy jumps with a two-stride run-up are advisable. It is important always to attempt heights that require a real effort, because low jumps will not call forth the same layout that is required at competition heights. It is permitted for a handkerchief or other marker to be tied to the bar as an aid to sighting. Some jumpers have a familiar high-point marked in their home at which they can aim their free leg both as a limbering exercise and a boost to confidence in their ability to clear great heights. Some jumpers also find that wearing a shoe on the take-off foot only, gives them more freedom to get their free leg up.

Points to watch in the layout are many. The trunk and head should be hoisted vertically because their weight will otherwise drop on to the bar by the rotation initiated by the swing of the free leg from the point of take-off. The most common error is in anticipating the layout and hence losing vertical elevation. When, in the case of a left-footed take-off, the right foot and arm have topped the bar, the left arm must be tucked into the side. The trailing leg, the last limb to cross the bar, is astride until the bulk of the body weight has begun to descend. In order to get it clear, it must be lifted and turned outwards so that the foot does not brush the bar off.

Attention should be given in training to the amount of work which precedes optimum performance because this will suggest the best distribution of effort in competition, including the best height at which to start and the number of jumps needed to warm-up for it. Constant warmth is essential for good jumping and since a track suit is perhaps too cumbersome, a pair of tights can be worn if the weather is cold. The knack of relaxing warmly clad between jumps should be cultivated. Tired muscles are not only weaker but less skilful in performance.

Month 1

Training programme for one week.

1st day. Free running 20 mins or alternative sport such as basketball.

2nd day. Jumping practice, weight or circuit training.

3rd day. Jumping practice, free running.

4th day. Weight or circuit training.

5th day. Full track session with jumping practice, followed by sprints with intervals in company.

Month 2

Training programme for one week.

1st day. Jumping practice and sprint work.

2nd day. Weight or circuit training.

3rd day. Jumping practice for near maximum height.

4th day. Weight or circuit training.

5th day. Sprint or other work only.

Weight training should be maintained during the season but confined to days well-removed from competition. Jumpers often take two or three days rest before competing.

On the day of competition. Arrange to be at the ground at least one hour before you are due to jump. Collect your number and ascertain the qualifying conditions if there are to be preliminaries. Note your place in the jumping order so that you can prepare in good time for each attempt without a last-minute struggle to strip. Warm-up and measure your run-up with care. Take the early jumps on a slightly different approach from your usual one so that the surface is unbroken for your more difficult trials. Relax between attempts warmly wrapped, studying the performance of rivals and building a resolve to win. After each trial, check your take-off point and adjust the run-up if necessary. Keep a record of your clearances and failures and plan your subsequent week's training with the object of improving next time.

POLE VAULT

U.S. CHAMPION	George N. Davies (at Boulder, Colo., 1961) 15 ft. 10 ¼ in.
EMPIRE CHAMPION	Geoff Elliott (England) 13 ft. 8 in.
EUROPEAN CHAMPION	Eeles Landstrom (Finland) 14 ft. 9 in.
OLYMPIC CHAMPION	Don Bragg (U.S.A.) 15 ft. 5 in.

Of the few athletes intrepid enough to attempt pole vaulting in the nineteenth century, the name R. D. Dickinson stands out as the performer of a world's best of 11 ft. 9 in. for England in 1891. This height was never scaled in early Olympiads though Americans were on top as they have been without fail throughout Olympic history. The pioneer of modern vaulting was perhaps Frank Foss who in 1920 set a world record of 13 ft. 5 in. in winning the Antwerp Olympic title. A Norwegian, Charles Hoff, attained the distinction of being the only person to disturb American domination of world lists in official history when he surmounted 13 ft. 11¼ in. in 1925. The long-awaited human 'ultimate' of 14 ft. was scaled in 1927 by Sabin Carr of Yale University who like the greatest champions collected Olympic honours, too, a year later.

Experts were forced to revise their quoted limits during the next decade. Lee Barnes, the 1924 Olympic champion, notched a world record of 14 ft. 1½ in. before losing his Olympic title to Carr. Then in 1932 Bill Graber topped 14 ft. 4⅜ in. for a two-year reign being succeeded by K. S. Barnes. In 1936 the youthful Earle Meadows became Olympic champion at Berlin and within ten months had set a world record of 14 ft. 11 in. shared in the same contest with Bill Sefton. The same year the so-called 'heavenly twins' tied for the American title with George Varoff whose world record they had broken, and with Cornelius Warmerdam. The latter took a further three years to develop the virtuosity which was to take him literally to unheard of heights of over 15 ft., culminating in 1942 with a prodigious clearance of 15 ft. 7¾ in. This mark defied for fifteen years the assaults of all-comers including the only vaulter in history to retain his Olympic title, the Rev. Bob Richards (1952 and 1956). Bob Gutowski, who finally raised Warmerdam's record in 1957 had a best height of 15 ft. 9¾ in. which was disallowed because his pole fell under the crossbar. The official record of half an inch less stood in the name of Don Bragg, the Olympic gold medallist. The 1961 record of George Davies from Oklahoma State College is 15 ft. 10¼ in., making 16 ft. seem not only possible but probable.

The archaic English record of Dickinson was unsurpassed until L. T. Bond went higher in 1928 and further improved to 12 ft. 7½ in. in 1931. F. R. Webster effected a series of elevations in 1936, the topmost being 13 ft. 1⅜ in. which bracketed him with ten other vaulters for sixth place in the Olympic final. Norman Gregor cleared 13 ft. 6in. in 1951 but this was not allowed as a British record as he was a reinstated professional having accepted small cash prizes at Highland Games competitions. Geoff Elliott equalled this mark and went on to make multiple improvements, his best of 14 ft. 1¼ in. receiving official ratification five times between 1954 and 1959. Elliott, the reigning Empire champion, was defending a title which he had won at Vancouver in 1954.

The qualities demanded of the good pole vaulter are manifold, and as with the high jumper, physical height is one of them. Warmerdam is 6 ft. 1 in. and Bragg 6 ft. 3 in. In addition, excellent all-round co-ordination, gymnastic ability and muscular strength in the upper body are essential. All pole vaulters are accomplished in routine feats of agility, such as cart-wheels and back-flips, and many are formidable rope climbers. The kind of explosive power seen in sprinters must therefore be combined with a high degree of innate physical cleverness to master the technique of vaulting. Bragg is about 14 stone in weight and a sprinter of even time pace, as was Warmerdam. Last but not least in the catalogue of requirements is patience: it has been said that it takes up to ten years to make a great pole vaulter.

Development of technique: vaulting has not, like jumping, evolved through a series of quite different styles. The essentials of good form have not really changed in the last thirty years. Improvements have to some extent been brought

about by better poles but mainly by perfecting and
strengthening the old movements.

The Rules: the uprights must be of rigid material and at
least 12 ft. apart. The pegs supporting the cross-bar must
project not more than 3 in. on the landing side and be not
more than ½ in. in diameter. The pole can be of any length

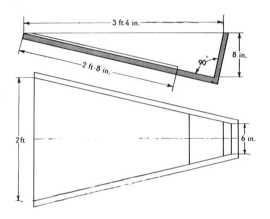

Figure 14

or size but if bound must have not more than two layers of
adhesive tape. The box in which the pole is planted must be
in accordance with the specifications shown in figure 14.
The competition rules for qualification and ties are the
same as in the high jump (*see* page 101).

In addition to dislodging the bar, the following constitute
failure on the part of the vaulter. Passing the plane of the
uprights without clearing the bar; touching the ground
beyond the box with the pole; leaving the ground as a
preliminary to attempting a vault; allowing the pole to
fall under the cross-bar; taking three approach runs without

vaulting; moving the lower above the upper hand, or the upper hand farther up the pole at take-off or later.

Equipment: the vaulter should have a sponge-rubber insert to ease the impact on his take-off foot. His pole may vary from 14 ft. to 18 ft. in length depending on the height and weight of the athlete. Bamboo or metal poles are frequently used but fibre-glass has proved to be the most flexible though the cost is prohibitive. It should be possible to graduate with improvement to the better poles, but the beginner will probably find that a metal one of 14 ft. is adequate.

Technique: though it is convenient to deal with pole-vault technique in phases, it is should always be thought of as a co-ordinate whole, beginning at the run-up and ending

Figure 15

in the pit. The components of this complex series of movements are the run, shift, plant, take-off, swing, pull, push, and drop.

The hold: figure 15 shows that the vaulter is facing

squarely in the direction of the bar. If he is right-handed, he will take off from his left foot and swing to the right of the pole. The pole is carried in the left hand and supported by the right; the arms are slightly bent to allow some free play for the shoulders and the hands as near together as is consistent with ease of carriage. The position of the right hand should be determined by measuring the height to be cleared with the pole standing vertically in the box.

The approach: the best vaults result from a run-up in which full speed has been achieved three paces from take-off.

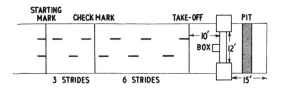

Figure 16

Most champions need about 40 to 45 yards to gain the kind of momentum that enables them to clear 14 ft. and more. The beginner will find about 30 yards enough to start with. Repeated runs on a track, with the pole, will help to establish a uniform stride pattern and provisional check marks can be noted. A suggested stride routine for a vaulter attempting about 10 ft. is shown in figure 16. The angle of the pole during the run-up should be about 30 degrees which is steep enough for ease of carriage without being too steep for an accurate plant in the box.

The shift: at three strides from the take-off, the left hand begins to slide back towards the right which is directing the pole to its destination in the box. The moment of impact in the box should coincide with the arrival of the left foot at take-off so that the accumulated impetus of the approach is applied to the pole which will elevate in an arc carrying the vaulter's weight with it.

The plant: the pole should be moved forward smoothly to the box, without reaching, and planted squarely in the deepest part of the box if possible.

The take-off: if the pole is under control, the arms should still be bent as the left foot leaves the ground. Opinion is divided as to the advisability of effecting a conscious stamp with the left foot, but it should certainly provide spring. At the point of leaving the ground, the hands are above the head and the forearms in a strong position parallel to the pole (Fig. 17).

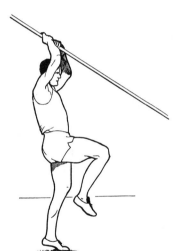

Figure 17

The swing: after take-off the body extends to full stretch with arms nearly but not quite straight. They must still be slightly bent for the pull. The body should swing behind the pole, using its momentum to assist the pole in its journey to the vertical. Only when the legs have swung past the pole should the pull-up commence. If the vaulter starts to heave from take-off, the timing of his effort will become deranged and he will impede the progress of the pole through its appointed arc. As the body closes with the pole, the hips are flexed and the knees raised (Fig. 18).

The pull: by now the momentum of the pole has slowed and the vaulter must utilize the remaining velocity to carry his centre of gravity across the bar. With the feet on a level with the head, the arms, which are still in a strong position

Figure 18

close to the pole, begin to hoist. The downward force of the pull combined with an upward thrust of the feet will achieve a position where the turn must be effected. The best way of turning is simply to twist the right foot in an anti-clockwise direction and it will automatically be followed by the right hip which should at this stage be high enough to surmount the bar.

The push: as the hands have not moved from the spacing of a few inches apart that obtained at take-off, they will still be in a strong position to complete the vaulter's climb to the summit of his trajectory and to simultaneously release the pole on the approach side of the bar. The landing has no hazards unless the vault has been badly timed. In a good sequence the body should plummet down feet first and fold at the hips on impact to achieve a comparatively relaxed backward roll.

Most faults in vaulting can be traced to lack of poise in the approach and take-off phases. It follows that the run-up and plant must be rehearsed repeatedly without a vault, the pole being released as soon as it is planted. The eyes must be kept on the box until after the plant and then raised to the bar, but the head should not be thrown back. The vaulter can adjust his check marks with the help of a friend, and like the hurdler, he will eventually acquire an eye for stride precision. Many pole vaulters actually include a little hurdling in their training to develop this.

Other phases which can be practised without going into the vault are the shift and turn. It is useful when warming-up for a session of vaulting to run up, plant, swing and turn into the pit without going for full elevation. None of the more crucial mid-air aspects of the vault can be mastered without complete confidence in the approach and plant.

Under the rules, the standards may be moved as much as two feet from the stop-board. At great heights, the bar is usually directly over the end of the box.

While early practices will be carried out with a hand hold at the same height as the bar, proficiency will enable the vaulter to clear heights of several inches above his grip. Warmerdam had a hand hold of 13 ft. 3 in. when clearing 15 ft. 8½ in. for an indoor world record. It is thought that further improvements in world standards will come from greater momentum in the approach making possible a higher hand hold.

If the take-off is correct the vaulter will have the feeling of following the pole in its arc both forward and upward and this should precede his pull-up effort. The double Olympic champion, Richards, has said that the essence of good vaulting is in the swing which must continue until the legs are past the pole. Only then should the pull-up commence. All the components of vault must be blended into a fluent whole which, as with any technique event, has a feel of its own that is the reward of patient application over a long period.

Training schedules: the pole vaulter's training can be conducted on the same lines as the high jumper's (*see* page 106). In addition he must spend time on building strength in the upper body and to this end weight training is invaluable. In the absence of suitable facilities, every workout should include some hard repetitions at such exercises as press-ups, chinning the bar, and sit-ups. More useful still is gymnastic work on ropes or parallel bars, and agility work on tumbling mats or trampoline. All this can help to vary the basic training particularly in winter, but as conditions permit, more time must be devoted to actual vaulting. Training at easy heights must form the bulk of practice for form, but not so low as to be a walkover. Vaulting for height should take place at least once a week, and if no competition is available, a training session should be arranged and carried out with full competitive thoroughness.

On the day of competition study the public transport to your venue and make sure that it will be possible to convey your pole with you. If not, make alternative arrangements. On arrival discover the qualifying conditions and warm-up in good time, setting your check marks and testing the pit. If it is unduly hard or not built up, draw the attention of officials to what may be a dangerous state of affairs. Conserve yourself in every way for a contest which may last for hours. Wrap up warmly between attempts. Do not be hurried, but strip as soon as the previous competitor has made his run and be ready to start as soon as the way is clear. Study your opponents and learn all you can from the afternoon's exercise.

BROAD JUMP (LONG JUMP)

U.S. CHAMPION Ralph Boston	(at Moscow, 1961)	27 ft. 1¾ in.
EMPIRE CHAMPION Paul Foreman (Jamaica)	24 ft. 6¼ in.	27 ft. 1¾ in.
EUROPEAN CHAMPION	Igor Ter-Ovanesyan (U.S.S.R.)	25 ft. 7¼ in.
OLYMPIC CHAMPION Ralph Boston (U.S.A.)	26 ft. 7¾ in.	

In the days before take-off boards the first man to clear 23 ft. was probably J. W. Parsons of Edinburgh University who did so by a scant ¼ in. when winning the 1883 A.A.A. title. Of the early Olympians, the most renowned was Alva Kraenzlein who added the long jump to his sprint and hurdle laurels with 23 ft. 6¾ in. in 1900. Only ½ in. behind him was another American, Meyer Prinstein who held a world's best of 24 ft. 7½ in. Prinstein took the Olympic title in 1904 but not before a lanky Irishman, Peter O'Connor had stretched his world record to 24 ft. 11¾ in., a landmark which stood undisturbed for twenty years, though approached by one centimetre by the 1912 Olympic gold medallist, Albert Gutterson.

In 1921 Ed Gourdin of Harvard leaped 25 ft. 3 in. but was defeated in the 1924 Olympics by another American negro, de Hart Hubbard. Both were however surpassed by a white American, Bob le Gendre, who reached 25 ft. 5¾ in. in the pentathlon competition at the same Games. Hubbard later improved to 25 ft. 10⅞ in. and even recorded one jump of over 26 ft. which was disallowed because the pit was one inch below the board. In 1928 Edward Hamm got within one inch of 26 ft. for a world record and collected the Olympic title at Amsterdam. In second place was a Haitian named Silvio Cator who rose to fame within weeks of the Games with a new world mark of 26 ft. 0⅛ in., a performance commemorated to this day on postage stamps in the island of his birth. Two inches were added to this record in 1931 by the nimble Jap, Chuhei Nambu, who a year later was to capture the Olympic triple jump title.

On the 25th May 1935 the announcer at a track meeting in Ann Arbor, Michigan, proclaimed that a new world long jump record was about to be set and spectators hushed while a handkerchief was placed at 26 ft. Seconds later the inspired feet of Jesse Owens parted the sand 26 ft. 8¼ in. from the board to launch a new superlative on twenty-five years of life. Owens did not attempt to improve on his first jump for he wished to resume the task of shattering world sprint and hurdle records of which he set three the same afternoon. The following year he took the Berlin Olympic gold medal with 26 ft. 5⅜ in., a mark which resisted the

attacks of the three next champions from America, Willie
Steele (1948), Jerome Biffle (1952), and Greg Bell (1956).
It was not until 1960 that Ralph Boston finally ended
Owens's reign with a jump of 26 ft. 11¼ in., which he
improved in 1961 to 27 ft. 2 in.

The English lists were distinguished in 1892 and 1893
by the presence of the name C. B. Fry, the Test cricketer,
whose best jump of 23 ft. 6½ in. not only eclipsed the native
record but equalled the then world's best. No Englishman
approached this target for thirty long years until Harold
Abrahams made the first of four improvements culminating
in a 24 ft. 2½ in. clearance on the eve of his Olympic sprint
victory in 1924. Abrahams's record was as durable as Fry's
for it was 1954 before Ken Wilmshurst made two breaks
through, the second of which earned him an Empire title
at Vancouver with 24 ft. 8¾ in. Roy Cruttenden added
exactly two inches to this record in a post-Olympic meeting
at Sydney in 1956 while in 1960, the spur of Olympic selection stimulated John Howell to a leap of 25 ft. 0½ in.

Sprinting and long jumping go together because the same
qualities of speed and explosive muscular power are
required for both. It is no coincidence that many of the
greatest long jumpers have been outstanding sprinters.
Owens's prowess has been mentioned and while Boston
has not reached the very top flight as a sprinter, he is capable
of 9.6 secs for 100 yards and has run 13.7 secs for the high
hurdles. Both he and Ter-Ovanesyan have been known
incidentally to clear 6 ft. 6 in. in the high jump. In addition
to cultivating jumping powers, the aspiring long jumper
must therefore study the section on sprinting because only by
developing his natural speed to the full will he achieve his
long-jump potential.

The Rules: conditions of competition should be printed in the programme and may consist of two alternatives. Jumpers may either compete for the best of three to six jumps, or, having taken three trials, the first three to six jumpers may proceed to attempt three more jumps. In either case, a competitor shall be credited with the best of all his trials. In the case of a qualifying competition having taken place at an earlier date or time, performances in the qualifying round do not register in the final reckoning. It will be recalled that in the Women's Olympic qualifying competition at Rome, Mary Bignal cleared a distance which would have gained her second place in the final, but since she was not among the best six ladies to qualify for three more jumps in the final, this performance was not taken into account.

The take-off board must be rigid and flush with the ground, measuring 4 ft. long, 8 in. wide, and 4 in. deep. The length of the jump is measured from the scratch line which is the edge of the board nearest the pit and this is often bordered by a sand or Plasticine filling to make it easier for judges to observe a jumper's foot overlapping the scratch line. A trial is registered if the jumper touches the ground with any part of his body beyond the scratch line, and if he touches outside the pit the jump is not measured though it still counts as a trial. The sand in the pit should be level with the approach and the board and if possible moistened or surfaced with a coloured powder to clarify the point at which the jumper breaks the sand. The pit should be at least 9 ft. wide and 20 ft. long with at least 10 ft. intervening between the board and the pit. Measurements must be taken to the nearest $\frac{1}{4}$ in.

Training for technique: long jump technique is simply the best way of converting ground speed into flight by means of a balanced take-off and terminating in a correct landing position. Methods of doing this have not varied greatly over the last thirty years, for the scope for artificial technique is necessarily limited by the straight approach. Again the long jump should always be thought of as a co-ordinated unit from the start of the run to the landing, but it is convenient as in the other jumps to describe the technique in phases.

The approach: the best jumpers vary in the length of their run between about 35 and 45 yards, the optimum being that which enables the jumper to attain the maximum speed that he can control in a balanced and well-directed take-off. Since a man's top speed is not reached until he has run 50 to 60 yards, the optimum long-jump speed is probably about 95 per cent of top speed. This running speed must be attained four strides from the take-off board so it follows that a high degree of stride precision in the run-up must be acquired. Figure 19 shows a suggested stride plan, and it is a good idea to practise the approach on a stretch of track without doing any jumping until accuracy in reaching a given

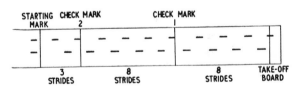

Figure 19

point in the right number of strides is developed. Unless the run-up is fluent, the take-off will not be reliable or balanced and impetus will be dissipated in shuffling adjustments.

The take-off: the objective here is to gain as much height as possible without checking forward momentum. The last four strides should be relaxed. This does not mean a slackening of speed but that concentration is on the take-off rather than on acceleration. The last involves a slight crouch and gather while the take-off foot is driven hard on to the board. With the body weight shifted over the take-off foot, the tendency to move it two or three inches away from the line

Figure 20

of running is natural but should not be exaggerated. This last stride is normally a few inches shorter than the previous one which assists the object of lifting the body-weight upwards from take-off.

In the air: the take-off foot drives the body up assisted by a concerted lift of the alternate knee, all this being a natural reaction of the impact with the board (Fig. 20). The lead leg then swings forward as if the jumper were running off the board, and then back again in a cycling action, to be thrust forward yet again together with the take-off foot as the legs extend towards landing. This style, known as the hitch-kick is the most effective. A modified version of this known as the hang involves identical action of the trailing leg, but no backward cycle of the lead leg which merely makes one forward thrust. In either case the timing of the trailing leg must not be hurried. It should fulfil its role off the board in a full drive from the hip, and come through to join the scissoring lead leg only on the downward flight.

The landing: with both legs extended almost horizontally forward with both arms, the heels break the sand, and the head and shoulders are hunched forward of the knees to lift the buttocks clear of the pit (Fig. 21). The jumper should then subside on to his hands and knees.

Training for condition: as sprinting is a fundamental component of long jumping, the jumper cannot do better than carry out basic training on the lines suggested for the sprinter in Part One, and in fact he should carry out some of

Figure 21

his training with sprinters at all stages of the season. Constant emphasis on exercises for spring is essential. Squat jumping will strengthen the knees and thighs which absorb so much of the impact of take-off. A sponge-rubber insert should always be worn in the take-off shoe and full effort from the board should be kept to a minimum to avoid the very real danger of damage to the heel and leg muscles. Low hurdling is a good exercise for stride precision which the long jumper needs in common with any other event requiring an even approach. Having warmed-up with sprinters the jumper should always build up to the high point of his training session with form exercises into the pit preferably from a grass take-off. Two of three easy jumps with a short run with special attention to knee lift at take-off, a few more with a leg scissor will complete his warm-up. Then, having rehearsed his run-up carefully several times, running through the pit to ease off, the jumper can finally get down to the flat-out jumping. This should be carried out as though for a competition with check marks noted and the track brushed clear after each trial. Six good jumps is a maximum and during the season even fewer should be attempted. This will preserve the jumping leg for competition when it will receive all the hard work it needs.

Training Schedules

The schedules for sprinting are a sufficient guide to the long jumper with, of course, work on jumping included three or four times in winter and perhaps twice a week during the season. The following is a suggested week's training for a long jumper during the season.

1st day. Thorough warm-up and work on jump form to remedy mistakes noted in the previous competition.

2nd day. Warm-up and starts with the sprinters. Low hurdling and finally a few good jumps for form if desired. Some jumpers prefer to practise their event only once a week in the season.

3rd day. Winders up to 150 yards and a few starts.

4th day. Jogging only, and some sprints.

It is most important to maintain exercises during the season in order to keep the jumping muscles in good tone at a time when little jumping in training is actually being carried out. Squat jumps, skipping and abdominal work such as raising the legs while hanging from a bar, are ideal.

On the day of the competition follow all the advice offered for a sprinter where it applies to you. Make sure you pack a tape to measure your approach and coloured pegs or powdered chalk for check marks. Take extra clothing; delays between attempts can allow you to cool off with fatal results to performance. Rehearse your run up several times before the competition and make any necessary adjustment. A significant wind may make a longer or shorter run necessary. Relax between efforts and remember that your best effort may well be your last so concentrate to the end. Note your performances and the amount of warming-up that preceded the best one. Learn all you can from your efforts and from those of your opponents.

RUNNING HOP, STEP AND JUMP
(TRIPLE JUMP)

U.S. CHAMPION   Ira Davis (at Rome, 1960) 53 ft. 10 in.
EMPIRE CHAMPION Ian Tomlinson (Australia) 51 ft. 7¼ in.
EUROPEAN CHAMPION Jozef Schmidt (Poland) 53 ft. 10 ¾ in.
OLYMPIC CHAMPION Jozef Schmidt (Poland) 55 ft. 1¾ in.

The hop, step and jump, as it is sometimes known, originated in Ireland where in 1888 Dan Shanahan cleared 50 ft. 0½ in. with the old and now illegal two hops and a jump style. Irish-Americans were responsible for the early twentieth-century landmarks, Dan Ahearne leaping a world's best of 50 ft. 11 in. in 1909 a year after his brother Tim had taken the Olympic title in London. Myer Prinstein the long jumper had taken the 1900 and 1904 Olympic titles with undistinguished performances, and it was not until 1924 that Ahearne's mark was erased by Australia's Archibald Winter who added a scant $\frac{1}{4}$ in. in winning the Olympic gold medal in Paris.

There followed a long ascendancy by Japanese jumpers who led the world in three Olympiads, Mikio Oda in 1928, Chuhei Nambu in 1932 and finally Naoto Tajima in 1936 with a superb jump of 52 ft. $5\frac{7}{8}$ in. This mark proved too good for all-comers until 1950 when Brazil's Adhemar da Silva started a series of improvements culminating in 1952 with an Olympic winning effort of 53 ft. $2\frac{1}{2}$ in. A $\frac{1}{4}$-in. improvement in 1953 by Russia's Leonid Shcherbakov kept da Silva out of the record books for two years, but he regained the summit in 1955 when winning the Pan-American title at Mexico City with 54 ft. $3\frac{3}{4}$ in. and in 1956 became the second triple jumper to retain an Olympic crown. The Soviet jumpers Ryakhovskiy and Fyedoseyev, both happily owning the more convenient first name of Olyeg, made marginal gains in 1958 and 1959, but it was the Polish prodigy Jozef Schmidt, who really revolutionised the event with an incredible 55 ft. $10\frac{1}{4}$ in. before going to Rome.

The short British history of the triple jump, which did not reach A.A.A. championship status until 1914, appears to have produced no noteworthy performers until 1923 when J. Odde cleared 46 ft. $4\frac{1}{2}$ in. Neglect no doubt accounts for the fact that 48 ft. was not surpassed until 1934. E. Boyce's jump of the 48 ft. $5\frac{1}{2}$ in. in that year stood for nineteen years. Ken Wilmshurst's career in the record books began in 1953 and developed by way of an Empire title at Vancouver in 1954, and several records to a best of 51 ft. $2\frac{1}{4}$ in. in 1956. Fed Alsop added 2 in. to this in the Rome Olympic qualification competition and a further $\frac{1}{4}$ in. in a late-season meeting in Berlin in 1960.

PART FIVE

Throwing

:chnical nature of the throwing events mak
st difficult to master yet in some senses tl
1g on the athletic programme. Though the
be the domain of the slow and cumbersom
:mand the best attributes of the sprinter ar
results are to be achieved. Explosive spee
oove all timing are needed if the maximu
to be imparted to the missile. The instructic
relates to right-handed throwers throughou
lless repetition, training schedules have bee
1e shot-putter only and it is hoped that th
fficient guide to the kind of training require
ing throwing events.

ration for all the throwing events will includ
vork on form, the thrower should always fin
work and if possible should go in for a
ort such as basketball which will help t
.eed and agility.

iscus and hammer are usually thrown frои
;, so rubber-soled shoes or basketball boot
worn by throwers in these events. In th
vith toe and heel spikes are advisable.

PUTTING THE SHOT

и Bill Nieder (at Walbut, Cal., 1960)
65 ft. 10 ii

PION Arthur Rowe (England) 57 ft. 8 ii

AMPION Arthur Rowe (G.B.) 58 ft. 4 ii

иPION Bill Nieder (U.S.A.) 64 ft.6¾ ii

130

The triple jump is a natural partner to the long jump and its exponents are athletes of similar type. The event is in fact a composite long jump requiring all the long jumper's qualities channelled into a similar but distinct technique. Speed is again a cardinal factor in success. Jozef Schmidt, a well-built 5 ft. 11½ in. and 12 stone, has run 100 metres in 10.4 secs and has long-jumped over 24 ft. 6 in. without special application.

The Rules: the first jump must be a hop, that is landing and taking off from the foot used at the take-off board. The second jump is a stride on to the other foot from which the third and final jump is made. If the ground is touched at any point between the three stages, the jump is invalid. A space of at least 35 ft. between the board and the pit should be allowed. In all other respects the rules for long jumping apply.

Training for technique: the crucial problem in triple-jump technique is achieving the optimum distribution of effort over the three stages which will permit of the greatest possible momentum carried forward and hence the longest aggregate result. It is certain that the dramatic improvements made in recent years have been the outcome of a new approach to this problem. Whereas the long-jump record has improved only 6 in. since before the war, the triple jump has elongated by more than a yard, clearly a much bigger proportionate advance. The following figures showing the intermediate measurements of great triple jumpers in history show how this modification in technique has come about.

Schmidt's first jump, it will be seen, was 16 in. shorter than Nambu's, yet his second was 2 ft. longer and his third nearly 4 ft. longer. This illustrates the way in which Schmidt mastered the art of placing only enough stress on the first

Year	Name	1st jump ft. in.	2nd jump ft. in.	3rd jump ft. in.	Total ft. in.
1932	Nambu	21 -	14 9	15 10	51 7
1936	Tajima	20 4	15 9	16 4⅞	52 5⅞
1955	da Silva	20 7	16 3	17 5¾	54 3¾
1958	Ryakhovskiy	21 2	16 4	16 11	54 5
1959	Fyedoseyev	21 3	15 9	17 9½	54 9½
1960	Schmidt	19 8¼	16 5½	18 8½	55 10¼

jump to facilitate the second and third, thus distributing his momentum to the biggest advantage over the triple jump as a whole. The approach to each stage of the triple jump should always be guided by its effect on the performance as a whole, but again it is convenient to deal with each stage separately on paper.

The approach: here all the considerations of speed, stride, precision, and control on the last three strides mentioned in the section on long jumping apply. The triple jumper can however adopt a lower angle of take-off since he is not concerned so much with height in his first jump. If he usually jumps from his right foot, it is almost probably best to use it first in here because it will certainly be his strongest leg and therefore best able to cope with the double impact of the first two jumps.

The first jump: the body-weight must be squarely over the take-off foot to permit a balanced flight and landing on the same foot. Assuming that the right foot is down first, the left knee is whipped up to hip level. The right leg then follows through to take the impact of landing while the left swings back to complete the scissor and counter the tendency to rotate forward. The right leg must swing back to provide a fulcrum and not reach forward at landing when it would have

the effect of a brake. The ba
the end of the first stride
co-ordinating thrust from th

The second jump: on land
and is whipped up bent at
ward. During this stride w
both arms are drawn back
take-off for the final jump.

The third jump: full con
to utilising the remaining
jump. The arms lift with th
to prevent the body overba
Generally the final jump is
kick with scissor, so the m
alternative long jump tec
best.

Training: obviously th
follow the same lines as
caution regarding possibl
this highly strenuous ev
carried out to build up t
strain of the third jump.
same leg for distances o
form of conditioning.

In competition, the a
relevant here. The tripl
competitive outings an
jump, low-hurdle, and s

THE highly
them the n
most rewar
often tend t
they in fact
jumper if r
agility, and
momentum
in this sectic
To avoid ne
outlined for
will form a s
for the rema

While pre
a lot of heavy
time for trac
alternative s
maintain his

The shot,
concrete circl
are commonl
javelin, shoes

U.S. CHAMPI

EMPIRE CHAM
EUROPEAN CH
OLYMPIC CHA

The first noteworthy shot man in twentieth-century history was Ireland's Denis Horgan who in 1900 set a record of 48 ft. 2 in. and collected thirteen A.A.A. titles over a span of nineteen years. The 280-lb. American, Ralph Rose, next held overwhelming supremacy with two gold and one silver medals in three successive Olympiads beginning in 1904, and a world record of 51 ft. in 1909. The name of Rose was perennial until 1928 when Germany's Emil Hirschfeld reached 51 ft. 9½ in. a mark which endured for only two months until Johnny Kuck heaved 52 ft. 0¾ in. for the Olympic title with the German third. Hirschfeld retaliated a month later with 52 ft. 7½ in. and this stood for four years, with one equaliser in the Czech, Frantisek Douda.

In 1932 Poland's Zelmut Heljasz held a brief ascendancy in the record books but was not prominent in the Los Angeles Olympics where Leo Sexton, a film Tarzan, came out on top with 52 ft. 6 in. Douda was third but had the belated satisfaction of regaining the world record the next month. Jack Lyman was responsible in 1934 for a throw of 54 ft. 1 in. starting an American domination of shot-putting records which has never faltered since. The first new entry on the lists came only six days later. Greatness was then personified by the 273-lb. Jack Torrance who threw first 55 ft. 1 in., then 55 ft. 5 in. and in August of that year, 57 ft. 1 in. This was the target of shot-men for fourteen years, and was nearly 4 ft. too far for the 1936 Olympic winner, Hans Woelke of Germany, with Torrance, by then an unwieldy 308-lb., occupying fifth place.

A modest throw of 45 ft. 8½ in. by T. Kirkwood in 1909 was unsurpassed in the United Kingdom for nearly two decades, the Cambridge blue 'Bonzo' Howland breaking the monotony in 1929 with 46 ft. and after a surprising interval of six years improving to 48 ft. 9 in. This defied renovation until the 6 ft. 7 in. Marine John Savidge commenced an irresistible progress in 1949 which took the record via seven increments to 55 ft. 2 in. in 1954, in which year he was Empire Champion. Barclay 'Tiny' Palmer had a brief tenure at 55 ft. 6 in. which terminated in 1957 with the arrival of Arthur Rowe. The most recent of Rowe's almost countless series of records is 64 ft. 2 in. which together with his Empire and European titles constitute a massive but probably unfinished catalogue of success.

World standards meanwhile had gone ahead more rapidly, Torrance's ultimate finally passing to the negro Charles Fonville, with 58 ft. $0\frac{1}{4}$ in. in 1948. Back strain kept Fonville out of the Olympics that year and the title went to Wilbur Thompson in only 56 ft. 2 in. In third place was America's James Fuchs who made three small increases on the world record before gaining another bronze medal at the Helsinki Games in 1952. There the prodigious Parry O'Brien took the stage with a gold medal throw of 57 ft. $1\frac{1}{2}$ in. to commence a long reign at the summit. O'Brien's world records punctuated the ensuing years at frequent intervals, the farthest being 63 ft. 2 in. in 1956 when he retained his Olympic title. The way seemed clear for him to effect another successful defence in 1960 but Bill Nieder, who had long lurked in his shadow, released an earth-shattering performance of 65 ft. 10 in. in August 1960 to become Olympic favourite and then Olympic Champion. O'Brien, like Ralph Rose in 1912, took a silver medal to add to the golden pair already in his collection. The bronze medallist Dallas Long, nudging 65 ft., is still however susceptible to defeat by the old master O'Brien.

Dynamical qualities of strength and speed are required of the successful shot-putter and these should be combined in an athlete of large proportions. Nieder and O'Brien, both 6 ft. 3 in. and about 240 lbs., together with Long, 6 ft. 4 in. and over 250 lbs., are an ample illustration of the shape and size of things to come in the shot world. Real strength is synonymous with speed because power in proportion to body weight makes for swift movement; sheer bulk is of no athletic value. It has been reported incidentally that O'Brien is capable of under 10 secs for the 100 yards which demonstrated the colossal momentum he brings to his shot-putting. Strength to these men means ability to lift weights and all have weight-lifting performances to their credit which command the respect of specialists with the barbell. Arthur Rowe (6 ft. 1 in. and 224 lbs.) does squats with over 500 lb. and the bench press with 300 lb., and these efforts are exceeded by the bigger Americans.

The rules: the shot must be 16 lb. in weight and 5 in. in diameter, spherical in shape and composed of solid iron or brass. The circle shall have an inside diameter of 7 ft. and be outlined preferably with an iron or wooden band raised about half an inch above the surface of the circle. The curved stop board, occupying the middle of the front half of the circle's circumference, shall be painted white and measure 4 ft. long, $4\frac{1}{2}$ in. wide and 4 in. high.

The shot must be put with one hand and arm from in front of the plane of the shoulders. The competitor's feet may touch the side but not the top of the stop-board and the shot must land within a 65-degree sector marked by lines radiating from the circle. The athlete must leave the circle from the rear half in a standing position.

In competition the best of six throws decides the result and ties are resolved on second-best performances. Measurements must be made with a steel tape to the nearest quarter-inch below the distance thrown.

Technique: little improvement in methods of shot-putting took place in the first half of the nineteenth century, the most dramatic technical advance having been made by O'Brien. His style is generally accepted to be the best. The object of this technique is to utilize every part of the body within the limitations imposed by the rules to impart the

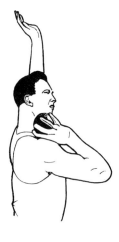

Figure 22

maximum impetus to the shot at the time of delivery. The sequence of movements must be thought of as a fluent chain of action which accumulates speed at every stage but again it is convenient to deal with the stages separately on paper.

Holding the shot: the shot should rest at the base of the fingers and receive lateral support from the thumb and little finger, with the wrist flexed. The loaded hand is then cupped over the collar-bone with the ball touching the neck and jaw (Fig. 22).

Taking the stance: a white line in the circle towards the direction of putting is a useful training guide. The right foot supporting the body weight is placed close to the rear border of the circle with the left foot poised easily behind it. The body is erect, the head in normal alignment, and the right elbow vertically below the shot. Perfect balance in this stance is essential to a fast and accurate glide.

The glide: the body bends forward at the hips countered by the left foot raised in the direction of putting. The left hand, head and shoulders overhang the rear edge of the circle to a point where the right elbow comes close to the right knee, at this stage flexed almost to allow the body to touch the thigh (Fig. 23). The right foot commences its thrust and simultaneously the left leg kicks backward along the line of putting. The thrust from the ball of the right foot is directed along the white line; the head has been kept at all

Figure 23

times in the same alignment and the eyes fixed on a pre-determined point directly behind the circle. Momentum is imparted to the shot as soon as the glide begins so there should be no check in the build-up of speed from this point.

Through the glide: the right foot leaves the ground at the heel but as the movement of the glide is horizontal, it should hardly raise at all. The tendency to turn the body should be delayed during the glide, the right foot only turning inwards to an angle of 45 degrees to provide a more direct thrust from the hip when the time comes. The right foot should stop and again support the body weight at about the half-way mark in the shift across the circle. The left foot comes to rest against the stop-board at which moment the shoulders and trunk which have hitherto faced the rear and not contributed to the shot's journey, begin their role in the accelerating sequence of delivery. Assisted by a drive from the still turning right foot, the trunk rotates. The putting arm adds the final stage of speed to the shot only when the shoulders have completed the 180 degree rotation which commenced at the beginning of the glide. This last thrust is less effective if initiated too early and must be applied only when the shoulders are square with the direction of putting. Following release of the shot, the body's continued rotation causes the right foot to follow through into the position near the stop-board occupied till now by the left foot which has quickly swung to the rear to counterbalance the tendency to overbalance out of the circle and invalidate the throw.

The technique of shot-putting can be practised at first in two main phases, the glide and the put, separately. The glide should be rehearsed repeatedly with special attention to balance and direction along the white line. Then several standing puts, with attention to rotation and late arm delivery can form part of warming-up for a training session. Training for form should always include some work on the full sequence at full effort to get the feel of the event as a whole.

Training for condition: easy running, limbering exercises and sprinting should be included in preliminary warming-up for every training session. The bulk of training for condition must however be devoted to building strength through weight lifting. Subsidiary sports such as volley ball, rope climbing or squash can be attempted perhaps once a week. The volume of work should not be allowed to slack off in the competitive season where six puts in competition are hardly enough exercise for a big man. For this very reason frequent competition is not recommended because it leaves insufficient time for training in the quantity that makes for real results. Experienced shot-putters often do fifty or a hundred puts in a single training session, but obviously this must be approached gradually and the number of puts regulated by the state of fitness. As the athlete grows stronger with weight training, he will correspondingly be able to hold his form for a longer period in practice from the circle. Strong muscles are both more enduring and more skilful.

MONTH 1

Training programme for one week.

1st day. Warming-up with sprinters, weight training.

2nd day. Putting for form.

3rd day. As 1st day.

4th day. Thorough warm-up as for competition and putting for distance until tired. Note number of puts taken to reach peak form.

5th day. Weight training or alternative sport.

MONTH 2

Training programme for one week.

1st day. Putting for form to remedy faults revealed by last competition.

2nd day. Limbering-up and sprints followed by weight training.

3rd day. Putting for distance.

4th day. Weight training.

5th day. Light track work or alternative sport.

The kind of training for a week in the competitive season should follow the lines of Month 2. The weight training should be maintained at least twice a week at all times.

On the day of competition (applicable to all throwing events), arrange to arrive at the arena one hour before your event. Report to the steward, collect your number and ascertain the qualifying conditions. If you are using your own implement have it approved by the appropriate official. Warm-up thoroughly taking several flat out puts if you have found in training that your best efforts follow plenty of practice. When taking the circle ensure that people are not walking across your immediate line of vision to the rear; balance depends on focusing on a fixed object during the glide. Study your opponents and learn all you can about the event.

THROWING THE DISCUS

U.S. CHAMPION	Jay Silvester (at Brussels, 1961) 199 ft. 2½ in.
EMPIRE CHAMPION	Stephanus du Plessis (S.A.) 183 ft. 6½ in.
EUROPEAN CHAMPION	Edmund Piatkowski (Poland) 176 ft. 10¾ in.
OLYMPIC CHAMPION	Al Oerter (U.S.A.) 194 ft. 2 in.

The discus was introduced to the first Olympic Games in 1896 by the Greeks to whom the event was traditional. They none the less failed to win it, this distinction going to an

American, R. S. Garrett, with the undistinguished throw of 95 ft. 7¾ in. A rare tie occurred at the 1904 Games when both M. J. Sheridan and the shot giant Ralph Rose threw exactly 128 ft. 10½ in., the former gaining the verdict on the throw-off and recapturing his title at London in 1908.

The discus event was not standardized as we now know it until 1912 when America's Jim Duncan set a record of 156 ft. 1¼ in. This proved impregnable for twelve years. In 1924 T. J. Lieb added a scant 1¼ in. after taking a bronze medal at the Paris Olympics. The champion on that occasion was Bud Houser, who was to push the world record out to 158 ft. 1¾ in. in 1926, and perform a successful Olympic title defence for the States in 1928.

English records were not officially listed until 1928 when the best available mark was the 126 ft. 1 in. propelled by M. C. Nokes of hammer fame in the previous year. K. H. Pridie made a modest advance to 135 ft. 6¾ in. in 1931 and was displaced by the Cambridge blue D. R. Bell who in 1936 managed 142 ft. 10½ in. An appreciable gulf was bridged in 1938 when a Scottish policeman, D. Young, hurled 153 ft. 8 in.

By this time the world had moved on to distances over 170 ft., Sweden's Harald Andersson being the first with 171 ft. 11¾ in. in 1934 and Germany's Willi Schroder following a year later with 174 ft. 2½ in. This stabilized the situation until 1941 when after a brief American tenure, the world record went to Italy's Adolpho Consolini. Consolini improved the record three times with an ultimate of 181 ft. 6 in. in 1948, becoming Olympic Champion in that year.

In 1952 a 6 ft. 6 in. American named Sim Iness beat Consolini for the Olympic title and the following year became the first human to throw 190 ft., passing that distance by half an inch. This was surprisingly shortlived for his compatriot Fortun Gordien, who had already held the record twice in 1949, now made two further improvements, getting one out to 194 ft. 6 in. Gordien was over the top by 1956 but even then took a silver medal behind Al Oerter, whose second gold medal at Rome made him the third Olympian in history to retain a discus title. Poland's Edmund Piatkowski took the world record to 196 ft. 6½ in. in 1959 but could finish only fifth at Rome. His record was exactly equalled in 1961 by Rink Babka, the Olympic silver medallist.

The United Kingdom record sustained no damage from 1938 to 1950, when John Savidge took time off from shot-putting to throw a discus 154 ft. 6½ in. H. I. Duguid came in with 155 ft. 3 in. in 1951 only to be surplanted by Savidge with a throw half an inch longer. These trivial exchanges were shortly outclassed by Mark Pharoah who contrived in three years to add more than 20 ft. to the native record, spinning a 178 ft. 0½ in. effort for fourth place in the 1956 Olympic final. More recent entries on the record lists have been supplied by Mike Lindsay and Gerry Carr, both recipients of American scholarships, the former having thrown 181 ft. 6 in., the latter 181 ft. 2½ in.

The discus requires strength, agility and co-ordination linked with good balance and timing. The great discus thrower must therefore have substantially the same qualities as the shot-putter channelled of course into an entirely different technique. The strong men of discus are all, it need hardly be stated, of large dimensions: Oerter is 6 ft. 3 in. and 224 lbs., Rink Babka, is 6 ft. 5 in. and 265 lbs., while Piatkowski, at 6 ft. and 220 lbs., is relatively delicate. A few athletes have combined shot and discus with notable results: O'Brien has thrown over 188 ft. with the discus, while among British athletes, Lindsay has supplemented his discus prowess with a 58 ft. shot-put. The two events go naturally together and most athletes will enjoy the variety that comes from using an alternative missile. They should not however lose sight of the fact that specialization ultimately produces the best results in either.

The Rules: the discus should weigh 4 lb. 6½ oz. and may be thrown in any way. The circle should be 8 ft. 2½ in. in diameter, other specifications and competition rules being as for the shot put. There is no stop-board.

Technique: after numerous developments in discus throwing in the twentieth century, the technique now commonly used, which can best be described as a revolving sling release, is accepted as the only effective method. Again it is convenient to deal with what is fundamentally one continuous action, in separate phases.

Holding the discus: place the hand flat on the discus in such a way that the tips of the fingers overlap the edge (Fig. 24). The grasp should ensure that on release the index

Figure 24

finger will be the last to lose contact because this helps to impart a smooth flight to the missile. The wrist should not be flexed.

The stance: the thrower takes up a position facing the rear of the circle with his back to the direction of the throw-

ing; in training it is useful to mark this direction with a
white line. A few preliminary swings of the discus with a
relaxed throwing arm will help the thrower to get the feel of
the platter.

Preliminary swings: the right arm swings once or twice at
shoulder level; in these swings the discus passes through the
maximum arc possible both behind and before the body,
and the shoulders should be moved freely to permit this.
The head and body are kept erect and the body weight
supported on whichever leg is beneath the discus, the
alternate leg flexing to facilitate easy rotation.

The turn: at the end of the last preliminary swing the
thrower begins to spin on the ball of his left foot over which
the body weight is poised throughout the turn. Having
turned a full 180 degrees in an anti-clockwise direction on
the left foot, the delayed right foot is raised and the leg
rotated from the hip bringing the right foot down to the
ground. As rotation continues the left foot is pushed out
towards the direction of throwing. Throughout this turn the
throwing arm has been held behind the back to leave the
greatest scope for movement in the delivery phase.

Delivery: when the left foot has halted the turn, the trunk
and shoulders, supported by a powerful drive from the
right foot and hip give impetus to the right arm which comes
through late for a whiplash delivery. (Fig. 25 shows footwork across the discus circle.)

In training, every opportunity should be taken of learning
about the behaviour of the discus in flight. Mechanical
principles applied to this problem show that the discus will
offer less resistance to the air if projected at an angle close
to the horizontal. This is because the air beneath it acts
against the force of gravity, delaying its return to the

ground. In practice the tendency will be to throw the discus at too steep an angle at first, and invariably this will result in the discus veering over and dropping abruptly to the ground.

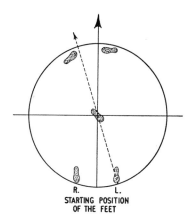

Figure 25

R.   L.
STARTING POSITION
OF THE FEET

When a wind is blowing, it is more than ever important to keep the angle of trajectory low because the effect of wind resistance on the surface of the discus is to accelerate its return to the ground. The discus is always more aero-dynamic when it knifes through the air edge-first. Its flight is not unlike that of a flat stone which can be made to skim the surface of water if thrown horizontally.

THROWING THE JAVELIN

U.S. CHAMPION   Al Cantello (at Compton, Cal., 1959)
282 ft. 3½ in.
EMPIRE CHAMPION   Colin Smith (England)233 ft. 10½ in.
EUROPEAN CHAMPION Janusz Sidlo (Poland) 263 ft. 0¾ in.
OLYMPIC CHAMPION   Viktor Tsibulenko (U.S.S.R.)
277 ft. 8¼ in.

The javelin throw as we now know it was first introduced to the Olympic Games in 1908 when Sweden's Eric Lemming won with 179 ft. 10½ in. Lemming regained his title at Stockholm in 1912 and soon after the Games improved his world record to 204 ft. 5½ in., this being the first record approved by the I.A.A.F. Jonni Myrrä of Finland followed Lemming's example by taking two Olympic gold medals in 1920 and 1924 and in throwing a world record of 216 ft. 10 in. The Scandinavian monopoly was given lustre in the twenties by E. H. Lundqvist, a Swede who won an Olympic gold medal in 1928 and soon after the Games let go a 232 ft. 11½ in. world record.

Javelin news was consistently made during the thirties by Finland's immortal Matti Jarvinen who set the first of his ten world records in 1930, a cast of 234 ft. 9¾ in. He then proceeded by way of the 1932 Olympic title to extend his best distance to 253 ft. 4½ in. in 1936 but was prevented by injury from successfully defending his Olympic crown. This went to Germany's Gerhard Stock with the modest distance of 235 ft. 8 in. In second place was a new Finnish discovery, Yrjo Nikkanen, who in 1938 was to boost his countryman's record in two instalments to 258 ft. 2 in.

Finnish supremacy in the Olympics was sustained after the war by the film actor Kaj-Tapio Rautavaara who won the Wembley javelin contest in 1948. His throw was far short of world's best however and this remained intact until America's Franklin 'Bud' Held got over the 260 ft. mark in 1953 and further re-wrote the record books in 1955 with 268 ft. 2½ in. Finland's last fling came in 1956 when Soini Nikkinen reached 274 ft. 1½ in. This was destined for only six days immunity from improvement, provided this time by Poland's Janus Sidlo at 274 ft. 5½ in. This too proved vulnerable when Sidlo went down in defeat to the Norwegian, Egil Danielson, who took the Olympic title at Melbourne with a magnificent world mark of 281 ft. 2 in.

In 1959 the American Marine, Al Cantello, added 13½ in. to the record but could finish only tenth in the Olympic Games at Rome. In eighth place was the luckless Sidlo, who had earlier brought off the farthest throw of the Games in the qualifying rounds. In ninth place was Italy's Carlo Lievore, who in 1961 made an astonishing leap to fame with a world record of 284 ft. 7 in.

English records were first listed in 1927 when a throw of 166 ft. 1¼ in. stood to the credit of W. P. Abell. Progress in the thirties was unsensational and it was not until 1939 that 200 ft. was surpassed; 'Hamish' McKillock managed 202 ft. 2¾ in. in that year. Post-war history was made by M. J. Dalrymple with 210 ft. 9½ in. in 1948. Mike Denley reached 216 ft. 1 in. in 1952, but was ousted within a week by Dick Miller throwing some 5 ft. further. In 1954 Miller got one out to 222 ft. 5 in. which secured his place in the record books for a further year. There followed a prolonged duel for U.K. supremacy between Peter Cullen and Colin Smith who each supplied four improvements during the next three years, Smith achieving a best of 246 ft. 7 in. in the Great Britain versus West Germany match in 1957.

Good javelin throwers are big and strong, though since the implement is lighter than either the shot or the discus, relatively small men have sometimes produced outstanding results. Carlo Lievore, at 6 ft. and 14½ stone, can be regarded as fairly typical of the good javelin athlete, while Al Cantello, the previous world record holder, is the exception at only 5 ft. 7½ in. and 168 lbs. The fact that modern javelins are more aerodynamic than the old wooden spears undoubtedly accounts for some of the advances that have been made in the last eight years, but they in no way form a substitute for skill. Javelin technique must be acquired in long and patient practice; the unskilled performer will get bad results whatever his implement.

The Rules: the throwing line is an arc of a circle of 26 ft. 3 in diameter and is normally marked by a strip of board or metal. The javelin must land within the sector bounded by two lines drawn from the centre of the circle and passing

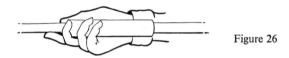

Figure 26

through the intersection of the throwing arc and the two lines bordering the runway. This should be 13 ft. 1½ in. wide and not more than 120 ft. long.

The javelin must be of metal or wood, circular in section and having its centre of gravity between 2 ft. 11½ in. and 3 ft. 7½ in. from the tip. The whipcord binding should cover the javelin for no more than 6¼ in. and should not exceed its circumference by more than 1 in. The javelin shall measure not less than 8 ft. 6⅜ in. in length and weigh not less than 11 lb. 12¼ oz. complete.

The javelin must be thrown over the shoulder with one hand and not slung or hurled in any unorthodox manner. A throw is not valid unless the point of the javelin strikes the ground first.

Technique: the object of technique is to impart the maximum impetus to the missile at the moment of delivery and to flight it at an angle calculated to keep it in the air as long as possible. These processes are set in motion by a correct approach run blended into the whiplash movement of release.

The grip: the javelin is rested in the palm of the hand with the index finger pointing towards the rear and the thumb and second finger behind the binding (*see* Fig. 26).

The run-up: between 14 and 17 strides are usual, the first 10 or 12 being used to generate impetus, the last four to assume a good throwing position. The javelin is held above the head and moved gently as the shoulders co-ordinate with the running action. The transition to throwing position is accomplished by a cross-step (*see* Fig. 27) when speed has been accumulated. The right arm is drawn down and back with the javelin, the left arm also comes across the body to permit a full sideways turn. The right leg receives the weight of the body with the foot turned outwards, and

Figure 27

the left leg, completing a full stride, is used as a brake from heel to toe. It is important to have both heel and toe spikes whether throwing from a cinder surface, which is preferable, or a grass surface.

The delivery: the braced left leg halts the forward progress of the athlete but his impetus still carries forward over the fulcrum of his legs. He must utilize this to the fullest extent now by giving a powerful thrust of his right leg, followed by his hip and shoulder. The javelin is always held back and only when the other co-ordinating forces have been applied

Figure 28

should it be pulled through in a final effort similar to the lash of a whip (*see* Fig. 28). The release should take place a few feet from the throwing arc to allow for the right leg to come through and prevent the athlete overbalancing to register a foul throw.

The severe and specialized stress of this event calls for great care in building up the muscles of the back and shoulder girdle in preliminary training, as well as attention to gradual warming-up before full effort. Standing throws are a useful method of rehearsing the sequence of movements in delivery and this can even be carried out indoors with the aid of a small pulley and weight. Great throwers have managed over 200 ft. from a standing position.

THROWING THE HAMMER

U.S. CHAMPION   Harold Connolly (at Walnut Cal., 1961)
230 ft. 9 in.
EMPIRE CHAMPION   Mike Ellis (England) 206 ft. 4½ in.
EUROPEAN CHAMPION Tadeusz Rut (Poland) 212 ft. 6½ in.
OLYMPIC CHAMPION   Vasiliy Rudenkov (U.S.S.R.)
220 ft. 1¾ in.

Irishmen were 'kings' of the hammer from early times. J. J. Flanagan was Olympic champion in 1900 and 1904 when a 9-ft. circle was used, and retained his crown in London in 1908 when the modern 7-ft. circle became standardized. His third winning effort was surprisingly better than the two previous and measured 170 ft. 4¼ in. Second to Flanagan in 1908 and like him an Irish-American was the mighty Matt McGrath, world record holder since 1907 with 173 ft. 7 in. McGrath took a gold medal and set an Olympic record in 1912, lapsed to fifth place in 1920, and then climbed to second again in 1924 at the venerable age of forty-six. The world record had been annexed in 1913 by Patrick Ryan with 189 ft. 6½ in. and it was Ryan who took the 1920 Olympic title at Antwerp.

The record lists were then undisturbed for twenty-five years but the task of winning medals still remained an Irish prerogative, Dr Pat O'Callaghan, a native of Cork, capturing the Olympic title in 1928 and resuming the mantle in 1932 at Los Angeles as a member of the two-man team who both won gold medals (Bob Tisdall won the 400 metres hurdles).

England's first hammer giant was Tom Nicholson who hurled 166 ft. 9½ in. in 1908 shortly after occupying fourth place in the Olympic final. M. C. Noakes made two impressions on this record in 1923, his furthest throw denting the turf at 173 ft. 1 in. The strong men of Britain had no answer to this until 1947 when Duncan McD. Clark made the first of three records, the last coming in 1950 at 183 ft. 9½ in., a few weeks after he had won the Empire Games title at Auckland. Dr Ewan Douglas, another Scot, and a close friend of Clark's, was good enough to supplant him in the record books with a throw of 192 ft. 6 in. in 1955. Only a year later, Peter Allday, a smaller man than his predecessors, generated enough speed in the circle to reach 195 ft. 7 in. In 1957 the United Kingdom hammer record was taken over by Michael Ellis and transformed via seven increments to its present level of 213 ft. 1 in. in 1957.

The world record of Pat Ryan was finally obliterated in 1938 by Germany's Erwin Blask, the Olympic silver medallist, throwing 193 ft. 6⅞ in. to establish a ten-year niche for himself. Hungarians took the first two post-war Olympic titles, Imre Nemeth succeeding at Wembley in 1948 and his pupil Jozsef Csermak coming out top at Helsinki in 1952 with a world record of 197 ft. 11½ in. Only six weeks after the Games, Norway's Sverre Strandli, who had occupied a modest seventh place at Helsinki, became the first human to throw 200 ft., passing that distance by 11 in. at Oslo. At the same meeting a year later Strandli sent his compatriots into raptures with another world best of 204 ft. 7 in.

The growing depth of hammer talent in Russia then threw up a new colossus in the person of Mikhail Krivonosov who demonstrated repeatedly that 200 ft. was merely a round figure. By 1956 he had collected a European title and taken the record up to 220 ft. 10 in. At the Melbourne Games however he met his match in America's Hal Connolly, who had already proved his metal with 224 ft. 10½ in. Connolly went on to pass another landmark in throwing 230 ft. 9 in. in 1960, but was off form at the Olympics to be beaten into eighth place.

It is emphasizing the obvious to state that hammer throwers are big men; Harold Connolly, at 6 ft. and 238 lbs. is typical, while Mike Ellis is taller than most of his rivals at 6 ft. 4 in., with a body weight of about 217 lbs. As the hammer is the most complex event of all technically, those who specialize in it seldom attempt other events. There is no instance of a world class hammer-thrower who has produced notable performances at any other throwing event. The fact that the hammer is a difficult skill makes mastery of it all the more rewarding for those who persevere. Ellis's dedication has given him a supremacy in his event which no other British athlete of the present day can claim; on the list of British best performances of all time, his name appears thirty-nine times before that of the second best performer.

The Rules: the circle shall be 7 ft. in diameter and outlined preferably by a band of wood or metal. The hammer shall weigh not less than 16 lb. and be not more than 4 ft. in overall length; its head should be spherical, the handle must be a single length of wire, not less than $\frac{1}{8}$ in. in diameter and looped at the end; it should be connected to the head by means of a swivel and to the grip by means of a loop.

The hammer must land in a 60-degree sector marked on the arena. The thrower must leave the circle from the rear half after the hammer has landed. Distance shall be measured from the near edge of the indentation to the inner edge of the circle.

A specially constructed cage usually encloses the throwing circle to ensure that inaccurate throws are trapped. Regular examination of the hammer will forestall another possible source of danger from an erratic missile.

Technique: though great strength must contribute to outstanding performances, it is not important for a beginner to think too much in terms of strength. The essential thing

Figure 29

is to groove the correct sequence of movements so that as bodily strength and fitness are acquired, they will be channelled into the most efficient method of propulsion.

The distance thrown will depend on the speed attained by the hammer head before delivery, and this will be at its greatest only if the head travels through the correct path in the swings. If the athlete's shoulders are the centre of the revolving wheel of which the hammer head represents the outer rim, the ultimate speed of the hammer will be at its maximum only if the path of the hammer is at right angles to the vertical. The optimum position for the trunk is therefore an erect one with the knees flexed for greater mobility in the turns.

The grip: the bar of the grip rests on the middle joint of the left hand on which a leather glove is worn. The right hand is placed over the left with its fingers covering the knuckles of the left hand. The grasp should not involve a tight pressure of the fingers (Fig. 29).

The stance: the athlete stands with his back to the direction of throwing, his feet at shoulder-width apart, body erect and knees flexed. Before going into the preliminary swings, the hammer should be placed on the ground to the thrower's right side and far enough behind him that his left arm and the wire form a straight line; the body must be turned at the trunk and the left knee bent and left heel raised from the ground to enable him to attain this starting position (Fig. 30).

Preliminary swings: the right arm lifts the hammer from the ground in a wide sweeping anti-clockwise direction at

Figure 30

an angle of about 45 degrees. The feet do not move but the knees flex to allow the trunk to rotate with the hammer which swings over the thrower's left shoulder in an upward arc; the arms must not be more bent than is necessary to perform the swing behind the back for the hammer head acceleration depends on its travelling through the widest arc. The trunk should be upright at all times and the eyes following the path of the hammer head from the ground to its highest point on his left. Two or three swings are usually taken and it is important to perfect these before learning the footwork of the turns.

The turns: three turns are almost universal, though Harold Connolly has developed a technique with four turns. The following remarks assume that the thrower is taking the orthodox three. Having completed the preliminary swings, the thrower starts to swivel on the heel of his left foot as the hammer passes his right foot, and raising his right heel, he spins through 180 degrees to the left. For the second half of the turn, the body weight continues to revolve on the ball of the left foot while the right foot leaves the ground, and turning with the body but remaining always low, returns to the ground in the astride position with a full 360 degrees turn executed. The athlete will now be facing the rear having moved about eighteen inches across the circle in the direction of throwing. The second turn follows without a break in the smooth and accelerating flow of movement, and third brings the thrower to the point of delivery. In each turn, the thrower is pulling the hammer to its high point and being pulled by it to its low point. This shift of emphasis is essential to the achievement of continuous acceleration throughout the series of turns, for if the body's rotation tends to catch up with the hammer it will not be in a position to do any work.

The delivery: at the end of the third turn the moment of delivery arrives as the hammer is reaching its highest point. Here the thrower's body must be turning ahead of the hammer to commence the series of thrusts from the legs, hips and body which will culminate in the final release from the left hand. The hammer leaves the thrower's gloved hand slightly above his left shoulder. The twist of this trunk will have caused his legs to be crossed at this point. Having parted with the hammer, it is now possible to move the right foot round and prevent himself from toppling out of the circle by completing his turn.

As an event which some regard as the most technically difficult on the athletic programme, it is important for the hammer-thrower to train in company. Throwers working together can pin-point each other's faults and introduce an element of competition which, without necessarily being overdone, can prevent them from becoming lazy. Hammer men must train regularly for strength with weights and resistance exercises, but this should not be allowed to supersede training for technique. The two should progress together so that the strength acquired is channelled into the correct technique.

Index

I EVENTS

II NAMES

158 INDEX